1st Celtic Language Technology Workshop

(CLTW 2014)

Held at COLING 2014

Dublin, Ireland
23 August 2014

ISBN: 978-1-63439-216-7

Printed from e-media with permission by:

Curran Associates, Inc.
57 Morehouse Lane
Red Hook, NY 12571

Some format issues inherent in the e-media version may also appear in this print version.

Printed by Curran Associates, Inc. (2014)

Association for Computational Linguistics
209 N. Eighth Street
Stroudsburg, Pennsylvania 18360

Phone: 1-570-476-8006
Fax: 1-570-476-0860

acl@aclweb.org

Additional copies of this publication are available from:

Curran Associates, Inc.
57 Morehouse Lane
Red Hook, NY 12571 USA
Phone: 845-758-0400
Fax: 845-758-2634
Email: curran@proceedings.com
Web: www.proceedings.com

Introduction

Language Technology and Computational Linguistics research innovations in recent years have given us a great deal of modern language processing tools and resources for many languages. Basic language tools like spell and grammar checkers through to interactive systems like Siri, as well as resources like the Trillion Word Corpus, all fit together to produce products and services which enhance our daily lives.

Until relatively recently, languages with smaller numbers of speakers have largely not benefited from attention in this field. However, modern techniques in the field are making it easier to create language tools and resources from fewer resources in a faster time. In this light, many lesser spoken languages are making their way into the digital age through the provision of language technologies and resources.

The Celtic Language Technology Workshop (CLTW) series of workshops provides a forum for researchers interested in developing NLP (Natural Language Processing) resources and technologies for Celtic languages. As Celtic languages are under-resourced, our goal is to encourage collaboration and communication between researchers working on language technologies and resources for Celtic languages.

Welcome to the First Celtic Language Technology Workshop. We received 15 submissions, and after a rigorous review process, accepted 12 papers. Eight of which will be presented as oral presentations and 4 of which will be presented at the poster session.

Organising Committee:

John Judge, Centre for Global Intelligent Content (CNGL), Dublin City University

Teresa Lynn, Centre for Global Intelligent Content (CNGL), Dublin City University

Monica Ward, National Centre for Language Technology (NCLT), Dublin City University

Brian Ó Raghallaigh, Fiontar, Dublin City University

Program Committee:

Steven Bird, University of Melbourne, Australia
Aoife Cahill, Educational Testing Service (ETS), USA
Andrew Carnie, University of Arizona, USA
Jeremy Evas, Cardiff University, Wales
Mikel Forcada, Universitat d'Alacant, Spain
John Judge, CNGL, Dublin City University, Ireland
Teresa Lynn, CNGL, Dublin City University, Ireland
Ruth Lysaght, Université de Bretagne Occidentale, France
Neasa Ní Chiaráin, Trinity College Dublin, Ireland
Brian Ó Raghallaigh, Fiontar, Dublin City University, Ireland
Delyth Prys, Bangor University, Wales
Kevin Scannell, St. Louis University, USA
Mark Steedman, University of Edinburgh, Scotland
Nancy Stenson, University College Dublin, Ireland
Francis Tyers, Universitetet i Tromso, Norway
Elaine Uí Dhonnchadha, Trinity College Dublin, Ireland
Monica Ward, NCLT, Dublin City University, Ireland
Pauline Welby, CNRS, Université de Provence, France

Invited Speakers:

Kevin Scannell, St. Louis University, USA
Elaine Uí Dhonnchadha, Trinity College Dublin, Ireland

Sponsor:

Transpiral `http://www.transpiral.com`

Table of Contents

Conference Programme

23rd August 2014

+	Opening
09.00-09.30	Invited Talk by Elaine Uí Dhonnchadha
	(09.30-10.00) Morning Session 1
09.30–09.50	*Developing an Automatic Part-of-Speech Tagger for Scottish Gaelic* William Lamb and Samuel Danso
09.50–10.10	*Using Irish NLP resources in Primary School Education* Monica Ward
10.10–10.30	*Tools facilitating better use of online dictionaries: Technical aspects of Multidict, Wordlink and Clilstore* Caoimhin O Donnaile
	(10.30-11.00) Break
	(11.00-12.30) Morning Session 2
11.00–11.20	*Processing Mutations in Breton with Finite-State Transducers* Thierry Poibeau
11.20–11.40	*Statistical models for text normalization and machine translation* Kevin Scannell
11.40–12.00	*Cross-lingual Transfer Parsing for Low-Resourced Languages: An Irish Case Study* Teresa Lynn, Jennifer Foster, Mark Dras and Lamia Tounsi
12.00-12.30	TBA

23rd August 2014 (continued)

(12.30-14.00) Lunch

14.00-14.30 Invited Talk by Kevin Scannell

(14.30-15.30) Afternoon Session

14.30–14.50 *Irish National Morphology Database: a high-accuracy open-source dataset of Irish words*
Michal Boleslav Měchura

14.50–15.10 *Developing further speech recognition resources for Welsh*
Sarah Cooper, Dewi Jones and Delyth Prys

(15.10-15.30) Poster Boasters

(15.30-16.00) Break

(16.00-17.00) Poster/Networking Session

gdbank: The beginnings of a corpus of dependency structures and type-logical grammar in Scottish Gaelic
Colin Batchelor

Developing high-end reusable tools and resources for Irish-language terminology, lexicography, onomastics (toponymy), folkloristics, and more, using modern web and database technologies
Brian Ó Raghallaigh and Michal Boleslav Měchura

DECHE and the Welsh National Corpus Portal
Delyth Prys, Dewi Jones and Mared Roberts

Subsegmental language detection in Celtic language text
Akshay Minocha and Francis Tyers

17.00-17.05 Closing

Developing an Automatic Part-of-Speech Tagger for Scottish Gaelic

Samuel Danso
Celtic and Scottish Studies
University of Edinburgh EH8 9LD
sdanso@staffmail.ed.ac.uk

William Lamb
Celtic and Scottish Studies
University of Edinburgh EH8 9LD
w.lamb@ed.ac.uk

Abstract

This paper describes an on-going project that seeks to develop the first automatic PoS tagger for Scottish Gaelic. Adapting the PAROLE tagset for Irish, we manually re-tagged a pre-existing 86k token corpus of Scottish Gaelic. A double-verified subset of 13.5k tokens was used to instantiate eight statistical taggers and verify their accuracy, via a randomly assigned hold-out sample. An accuracy level of 76.6% was achieved using a Brill bigram tagger. We provide an overview of the project's methodology, interim results and future directions.

1 Introduction

Part-of-speech (PoS) tagging is considered by some to be a solved problem (cf. Manning, 2011: 172). Although this could be argued for languages and domains with decades of NLP work behind them, developing accurate PoS taggers for highly inflectional or agglutinative languages is no trivial task (Oravecz and Dienes, 2002: 710). Challenges are posed by the profusion of word-forms in these languages – leading to data sparseness – and their typically complex tagsets (*ibid.*). The complicated morphology of the Celtic languages, of which Scottish Gaelic (ScG) is a member,[1] led one linguist to state, "There is hardly a language [family] in the world for which the traditional concept of 'word' is so doubtful" (Ternes, 1982: 72; cf. Dorian, 1973: 414). As inauspicious as this may seem for our aims, tagger accuracy levels of 95-97% have been achieved for other morphologically complex languages such as Polish (Acedański, 2010: 3), Irish (Uí Dhonnchadha and Van Genabith, 2006) and Hungarian (Oravecz and Dienes, 2002: 710). In this paper, we describe our effort to build – to the best of our knowledge – the first accurate, automatic tagger of ScG.

Irish is the closest linguistic relative to Gaelic in which substantial NLP work has been done, and Uí Dhonnchadha and Van Genabith's work (2006; cf. Uí Dhonnchadha, 2009) provides a valuable reference point. For them, a rule-based method was the preferred option, as a tagged corpus of Irish was unavailable (Uí Dhonnchadha, 2009: 42).[2] They used finite-state transducers for the tokenisation and morphological analyses, and context-sensitive Constraint Grammar rules to carry out PoS disambiguation (2006: 2241). In our case, after consultation, we decided to adopt a statistical approach. We were motivated by the availability of a pre-existing, hand-tagged corpus of Scottish Gaelic (see Lamb, 2008: 52-70), and our expectation that developing an accurate, rule-based tagger would take us beyond our one-year timeframe.

2 Methodology

2.1 Annotation

Using an adapted form of the PAROLE Irish tagset (Uí Dhonnchadha, 2009: 224), we manually re-tagged the corpus of ScG mentioned above. Significant conversion was required, as the corpus had been designed for a study of register variation (Lamb, 2008). Currently, 13.5k tokens have been final-

[1] The Goidelic branch includes Scottish Gaelic, Irish and Manx Gaelic. Welsh, Breton and Cornish are part of the Brythonic branch.

[2] Uí Dhonnchadha (2009: 213; cf *ibid*: 42) states her future intention to induce a Brill tagger on a Gold-standard corpus of Irish.

Proceedings of the First Celtic Language Technology Workshop, pages 1–5,
Dublin, Ireland, August 23 2014.

ised and used to train and evaluate various tagger algorithms, as described below. Our motivations for adapting the Irish tagset were to facilitate comparisons between Irish and ScG corpora, and to follow emergent *de facto* standards, as recommended in Leech (2005). Although this expedited progress, some tokens could not be easily classified.

Like Irish (cf. Uí Dhonnchadha, 2009: 81), ScG morphology is generally regarded as complex, particularly in the nominal system. Various process can re-shape word-forms, resulting in data sparseness; sparsity is a common issue in NLP work with morphologically-rich languages (Orvecz and Dienes, 2002: 711). These processes include initial consonant mutation (e.g. *c* → *ch*); internal vowel change (e.g. *a* → *oi*); palatalisation of final consonants (e.g. *-at* → *-ait*) and affixation. For example, the singular noun *cearc* ['hen'] declines for case and definiteness as *cearc, chearc, circ, chirc, circe* and *chirce.* The adjective *mall* ['slow'] can be found variably as *mall, mhall, malla, mhalla, moill, mhoill, moille* and *mhoille.*[3] To compound issues, as the language attrites, historically robust distinctions are being levelled or inconsistently observed. Another obstacle was ambiguous function words, such as *a* and *a'*; these can be tagged in various ways,[4] depending on context. There were also a small number of fused forms having multiple grammatical categories: e.g. *cuimhneam* ['I know'],[5] ← *cuimhne* ['knowledge'] + *agam* ['at me']. It was not possible, in all cases, to split these at the tokenisation stage and introducing further complexity to an already involved tagset seemed ill-advised. Therefore, we determined to use concatenation tags (cf. Chungku et al., 2010: 105), e.g. *cuimhneam* ['knowledge at me'] <Ncsfn+Pr1s>. This tag is glossed as: Noun common singular feminine nominative + Pronoun prepositional 1st-person singular.

2.2 Tokenisation

A full account of the automatic tokeniser is beyond the scope of this paper. What follows is a brief description of our guiding principles and the manual tokenisation of the training corpus. As a rule, we strove for a 1:1 correspondence between words/punctuation and tokens (1). However, some exceptions were necessary. As illustrated in (2) by the phrase *mu dheireadh* ['at last'], multi-word expressions were tokenised together when they performed an indivisible grammatical function[6] and could not be intersected by another word. Here, we took a slightly different approach from Uí Dhonnchadh (2009: 71-72); our preference was for a low number of MWEs in order to avoid the need for a complicated lexicon.[7] In a few cases, we split words into two or more tokens if a failure to have done so would have negatively impacted the pipeline further on (e.g. during lexicon extraction). In (3), this is illustrated by the word *dh'fhuirich* ['stayed'], which has been split into two tokens, separating the morphophonemic particle *dh'* from the verbal form. As described in Uí Dhonnchadha (2009: 70-71), this obviates duplication in the lexicon (cf. *m'ad*$_1$ ['my hat'] → *m'*$_1$ *ad*$_2$).

1) 1 WORD → 1 TOKEN
“$_1$*Ò*$_2$ *cha*$_3$ *robh*$_4$ *e*$_5$ *seo*$_{6,7}$*”*$_8$ *ars'*$_9$ *ise*$_{10}$ → *"*$_1$ *Ò*$_2$ *cha*$_3$ *robh*$_4$ *e*$_5$ *seo*$_6$ *,*$_7$ *"*$_8$ *ars´*$_9$ *ise*$_{10}$

2) ≥ 2 WORDS → 1 TOKEN
Bhàsaich$_1$ *am*$_2$ *fear*$_3$ *mu*$_4$ *dheireadh*$_5$ → *Bhàsaich*$_1$ *am*$_2$ *fear*$_3$ *mu dheireadh*$_4$

3) 1 WORD →≥2 TOKENS
Dh'fhuirich$_1$ *e*$_2$ *ann*$_3$ → *Dh'*$_1$*fhuirich*$_2$ *e*$_3$ *ann*$_4$

---

[3] See Lamb (2008: 197-280) for further details on Gaelic grammar. Many of the same issues are encountered in Irish (see Uí Dhonnchadha, 2009).

[4] The word *a*, for instance, can be variably tagged as a 3rd person masc possessive, a relative PN, a verbal agreement marker, the vocative particle, an interrogative pronoun, a simple preposition and a numerical counting particle.

[5] NB: *cuimhneam* is a fused form consisting of a noun and a prepositional pronoun. Like Russian, Gaelic expresses possession in a locative fashion (e.g. *tha e agam* ['I have it', lit. 'it is at me']; there is no verb of possession.

[6] As defined by the tagset.

[7] However, toponyms were tokenised as MWEs, e.g. *Dùn Èideann* 'Edinburgh' (cf. Uí Dhonnchadha, 2009: 72).

More generally, the corpus was manually divided into clauses, with each clause on a separate line. This was done to provide additional context for automatic tag disambiguation, with clause boundaries used in lieu of 'sentence boundaries' for instantiating the taggers. Clauses are linguistically well-defined structures, whilst sentences are not (Miller and Weiner, 1998: 71).

2.3 Tagger Instantiation

The PoS tagging task can be formulated as follows: given a word w_i, derived from a sequence of words ($w_i...w_n$), assign the best tag t_i, derived from a set of tags, $T=\{t_i..t_n\}$. After our 13.5k token sample had been manually tagged and twice verified, we used it to instantiate two stochastic taggers – bigram HMM (see Huang et al., 2009: 214) and trigram TnT (Brants, 2000: 224) – and a hybrid tagger (Brill, 1992: 112), which combines a stochastic and rule-based method. We employed the principle of *ensemble learning* (Dietterich, 2000: 1), whereby simple statistical PoS tagging algorithms can be usefully employed to improve the precision of more sophisticated algorithms. For comparative purposes, we also included simple unigram, bigram and trigram taggers. Simple n-gram algorithms tend to assign tags based on the most frequent tag sequence of the n-gram as observed in the training set.

On the surface, the HMM and TnT algorithms employ similar approaches to tagging, as both analyse the sequential history of word–tag pairings in a given 'sentence' using Markov Model principles (Ghahramani, 2001: 9). However, the approaches employed by HMM and TnT are somewhat different. HMM is based on first-order Markov Model principles, whereas TnT tends to be based upon second-order ones. Additionally, TnT tends to employ additional features during training, such as capitalisation and suffixes (Brants, 2000: 224). The Brill tagger, on the other hand, is an example of Transformational-Based Learning (Brill, 1992: 112). Like a stochastic tagger, it begins by pairing words with their most likely tags, as observed in the training corpus. This can be done using unigrams, bigrams or trigrams. It then notes where tags are applied incorrectly and attempts to induce corrective rules via various context-sensitive templates (*ibid.*: 113). Finally, it re-tags the corpus according to learnt patterns. A typical template is 'replace t_1 with t_2 in the context of C'. Some glossed examples from the Gaelic corpus follow:

1) **Ug** → **Q-r** if the tag of words i+1...i+2 is '**V-s**' [token = a]
Change the tag for the ***agreement marker*** *to one for a* ***relative pronoun*** *if one of the next two words is tagged as a* ***past-tense verb***

2) **Tdsm** → **Tdsf** if the tag of words i+1...i+2 is '**Ncsfn**' [token = a']
Change the tag for the ***singular, masculine definite article*** *to one for* ***the singular, feminine definite article*** *if one of the following two words is a* ***singular, feminine noun in the nominative***

3) **Sa** → **Tdsf** if the tag of the following word is '**Ncsfn**' [token = a']
Change the tag for the ***aspectual particle*** *to one for the* ***singular, feminine definite article*** *if the following word is tagged as a* ***singular, feminine noun in the nominative***

One of the advantages of the Brill tagger over other stochastic approaches is its transparency. With a knowledge of the tagset and target language, its output is easily understood. As seen in the above examples, it is capable of handling the problematic homographs discussed in §2.1.

Eight models, in total, were developed and assessed using the same training and testing set (see Table 1). Since the Brill tagger requires the output of a stochastic tagger before applying inductive methods, as described above, we employed the unigram algorithm as a base. Our ensemble strategy used a *backoff* mechanism, implemented as part of the Natural Language Tool Kit (NLTK) libraries (Bird, 2006: 70). Backoff creates a chain of PoS tagging algorithms that are executed in sequential order, ensuring that if an initial tagger is unable to classify a given token, then that token is passed on to the next tagging algorithm. Two ensemble-based models were developed: Brill (with bigram) and Brill (with trigram). Thus, in addition to using the simple unigram model as an initial stochastic tagger with Brill, we also employed bigram and trigram models. Brill (bigram) passes any untagged token to the unigram tagger, whereas the Brill (trigram), employs the bigram algorithm for untagged tokens and then passes any untagged tokens onto the unigram algorithm. In all cases, these stochastic stages are followed by the inductive of rules characterising the Brill algorithm. We used the default parameters of all algorithms, apart from one in the Brill algorithm, which defines the number of rules to be learned automatically from the training corpus. This was set to 150, as it optimised performance with the training set (NB: it did not apply to the test set).

We employed the hold-out method to evaluate our models (cf. Acedański 2010). To achieve this, we randomly divided the corpus sample into a 10% 'hold-out' set for evaluation (165 sentences, ~986 tokens), and a 90% 'training' set for model development (1492 sentences, ~12,560 tokens). We assessed the performance of the models by calculating the percentage of correctly assigned PoS tags for each against the manually assigned tags.

3 Results

The table below shows the preliminary results.

Table 1: Preliminary performance comparison of 8 statistical taggers

Model	*Unigram*	*Bigram*	*Trigram*	*HMM*	*TnT*	*Brill*$_{UNI}$	*Brill*$_{BI}$	*Brill*$_{TRI}$
Accuracy	66.1	52.1	23.6	74.6	76.1	75.6	**76.6**	75.2

As seen in Table 1, the most successful method, at present, is the Brill bigram model, which had a performance level of 76.6%. This is to be expected given the granularity of the tagset, along with the restricted training data; we expect accuracy to increase once we utilise the full corpus of ~86k tokens.[8] Unsurprisingly, due to sparsity issues, the least successful model was the simple trigram, at 23.6%. The performance of the TnT model was somewhat better than HMM (HMM: 74.6% and TnT: 76.1%), and also better than the Brill unigram model (TnT: 76.1% and Brill$_{UNI}$: 75.6%). The Brill bigram model, which is ensemble-based, outperformed the TnT model by about 0.5% (Brill$_{BI}$: 76.6% and TnT: 76.1%). There was, however, a drop in performance of about 1.4% between the Brill bigram (76.6 %) and Brill trigram (75.2%). Overall, our top accuracy level is comparable to that reported in Dandapat et al. (2007: 223) for their 10k sample (84.73%), although they experienced less sparsity as their tagset had only 40 categories (*ibid.*: 221).

4 Discussion and Future Work

In this paper, we describe an on-going project that seeks to develop the first automatic tagger for ScG. We employed supervised methods to develop and evaluate eight different PoS tagging models. Despite the promising results, more work is indicated. Data sparsity is the most likely explanation for the relatively low performance across the models. This is exemplified by the 43% difference between the performance of the simple trigram and unigram models. Considering the size of the our current training set (12.5k tokens) and the granular nature of the tagset (242 discrete categories), it seems unavoidable at present. The majority of tags had less than five instances in the training set, making it difficult for the algorithms to generate useful patterns. We will address this problem soon by including the full corpus, once it has been verified. Subsequently, we will carry out a fine-grained error analysis to determine which PoS features require further development. To improve results, we may integrate a limited amount of morphological analysis, as well a lexical database that has been made available to us (Bauer & Robertson, 2014). Finally, we will be exploring a multi-phase feature disambiguation scheme similar to that described in Acedański (2010: 5).

Acknowledgements

We would like to thank Prof Mirella Lapata (University of Edinburgh) for reading a draft of this paper and providing helpful comments. Many thanks to project members Dr Sharon Arbuthnot for retagging the corpus and helping to devise the tagset, and Ms Susanna Naismith for her work in verifying and

[8] Since this paper was written, the Brill tagger has achieved 86.8% accuracy (cf 92.5% on word classes only), using an 80k token training sample and 6,460 token test sample.

correcting the corpus. Finally, our appreciation to the Carnegie Trust for the Universities of Scotland and Bòrd na Gàidhlig for their generous financial support.

References

Szymon Acedański. 2010. A morphosyntactic Brill tagger for inflectional languages. *Advances in Natural Language Processing*. Berlin: Springer Berlin Heidelberg, 3-14

Michael Bauer and William Robertson. 2014. Am Faclair Beag (On-line dictionary). Available at www.faclair.com.

Steven Bird. 2006. NLTK: The natural language toolkit. *Proceedings of the COLING/ACL on Interactive presentation sessions*. Association for Computational Linguistics, 69-72.

Thorsten Brants. 2000. TnT: a statistical part-of-speech tagger. *Proceedings of the sixth conference on Applied natural language processing*. Association for Computational Linguistics, 224-231

Eric Brill. 1992. A simple rule-based part of speech tagger. *Proceedings of the workshop on Speech and Natural Language*. Association for Computational Linguistics, 112-116

Chungku Chungku, Jurmey Rabgay, and Gertrud Faaß. 2010. *Building NLP resources for Dzongkha: a tagset and a tagged corpus*. Paper presented at the Proceedings of the 8th workshop on Asian language resources, 103-110.

Sandipan Dandapat, Sudeshna Sarkar, and Anupam Basu. 2007. Automatic part-of-speech tagging for Bengali: An approach for morphologically rich languages in a poor resource scenario. *Proceedings of the 45th Annual Meeting of the ACL on Interactive Poster and Demonstration Sessions*, 221-224.

Thomas G. Dietterich. 2000. Ensemble methods in machine learning. *Multiple Classifier Systems*. Berlin: Springer Berlin Heidelberg, 1-15.

Nancy Dorian. 1973. Grammatical change in a dying dialect. *Language*, 49:413-438.

Zoubin Ghahramani. 2001. An introduction to hidden Markov models and Bayesian networks. *International Journal of Pattern Recognition and Artificial Intelligence*, 15(01):9-42.

Zhongqiang Huang, Vladimir Eidelman, and Mary Harper. 2009. Improving a simple bigram HMM part-of-speech tagger by latent annotation and self-training. *Proceedings of Human Language Technologies: The 2009 Annual Conference of the North American Chapter of the Association for Computational Linguistics, Companion Volume: Short Papers*. Association for Computational Linguistics, 213-216

William Lamb. 2008. *Scottish Gaelic Speech and Writing: Register Variation in an Endangered Language*. Belfast: Cló Ollscoil na Banríona.

Geoffrey Leech. 2005. In Martin Wynne (Ed.), *Developing Linguistic Corpora: a Guide to Good Practice*. Oxford: Oxbow Books, 17-29. Retrieved from http://ahds.ac.uk/linguistic-corpora [accessed 28 April 2014].

Christopher Manning. 2011. Part-of-speech tagging from 97% to 100%: Is it time for some linguistics? In A. Gelbukh (Ed.), *Computational Linguistics and Intelligent Text Processing, 12th International Conference, CICLing 2011, Proceedings, Part I*. Lecture Notes in Computer Science 6608. Berlin: Springer Berlin Heidelberg, 171-189

James E. Miller and Regina Weinert. 1998. *Spontaneous Spoken Language: Syntax and Discourse*. Oxford: Clarendon Press.

Csaba Oravecz and Péter Dienes. 2002. Efficient stochastic part-of-speech tagging for Hungarian. *The Proceedings of the Third International Conference on Language Resources and Evaluation (Las Palmas)*, 710-717.

Elmer Ternes. 1982. The grammatical structure of the Celtic languages. In R. Driscoll (Ed.), *The Celtic Consciousness*. Edinburgh: Canongate, 69-78.

Elaine Uí Dhonnchadha. 2009. Part-of-speech tagging and partial parsing for Irish using finite-state transducers and Constraint Grammar. PhD thesis. Dublin City University, School of Computing.

Elaine Uí Dhonnchadha and Joseph van Genabith. 2006. A Part-of-Speech tagger for Irish using finite state morphology and constraint grammar disambiguation. *Proceedings of the 5th International Conference on Language Resources and Evaluation (LREC 2006)*, 2241-2244.

Using Irish NLP resources in Primary School Education

Monica Ward
School of Computing
Dublin City University
Ireland
mward@computing.dcu.ie

Abstract

This paper looks at the use of Natural Language Processing (NLP) resources in primary school education in Ireland. It shows how two Irish NLP resources, the Irish Finite State Transducer Morphological Engine (IFSTME) (Uí Dhonnchadha, 2002) and *Gramadóir* (Scannell, 2005) were used as the underlying engines for two Computer Assisted Language Learning (CALL) resources for Irish. The IFSTME was used to supply verb conjugation information for a Verb Checker Component of a CALL resource, while *Gramadóir* was the underlying engine for a Writing Checker Component. The paper outlines the motivation behind the development of these resources which include trying to leverage some of the benefits of CALL for students studying Irish in primary school. In order to develop CALL materials that were not just an electronic form of a textbook, it was considered important to incorporate existing NLP resources into the CALL materials. This would have the benefit of not re-inventing the wheel and of using tools that had been designed and testing by a knowledgeable NLP researcher, rather than starting from scratch. The paper reports on the successful development of the CALL resources and some positive feedback from students and teachers. There are several non-technical reasons, mainly logistical, which hinder the deployment of Irish CALL resources in schools, but Irish NLP researchers should strive to disseminate their research and findings to a wider audience than usual, if they wish others to benefit from their work.

1 Introduction

This paper looks at how Irish NLP resources can be used in the development of Computer Assisted Language Learning (CALL) resources. It reports on the motivation for using CALL and specifically NLP/CALL in the primary school context in Ireland. Irish is a compulsory subject in primary schools in Ireland and most students spend 13 years studying the language (Murtagh, 2003), but it is not a particularly popular subject (Ó Riagáin and Ó Glíasáin, 1994, DCRGA, 2009) . CALL has many potential benefits for the language learner and it is important the students learning Irish have access to reliable, good quality CALL resources. However, it is difficult to develop such CALL resources, as usually a multi-disciplinary team is required, and such a team is often hard to assemble. One approach is to try to adapt and reuse existing resources to speed up the development process and indeed, provide resources that might not otherwise exist.

With this in mind, two existing NLP resources for Irish were used to develop CALL resources for students in the primary school context. The use of the resources is not limited to primary school students, but they were developed with these students as the target learning group. The first tool that was used was the Irish Finite State Transducer Morphology Engine (Uí Dhonnchadha, 2002). It was used to provide verb conjugation information for the Verb Conjugation Component (VCC) of the CALL resources. The aim of the VCC was to provide static and dynamic web pages with verb conjugation information and exercises/language games for the learner. The second tool used was *Gramadóir* (Scannell, 2005). It is a grammar checking tool and provided the underlying engine for the Writing Checker Component for the CALL resources. A wrapper was placed around *Gramadóir* in order to adapt it for the target learners. This included modifying the errors messages to be more young-learner friendly and separating spelling and grammar errors. CALL resources were developed using these

Proceedings of the First Celtic Language Technology Workshop, pages 6–17,
Dublin, Ireland, August 23 2014.

Irish NLP resources and deployed in two primary schools in Ireland. The students were able to use the resources without any major difficulties, but long term use depends on factors other than the NLP/CALL integration ones. However, in order to make use of the NLP resources that are currently available to CALL developers, it behoves NLP researchers to make their research widely available and comprehensible to a non-NLP knowledgeable audience. Of course, CALL researchers should also try to interact with the NLP community for a fruitful exchange of ideas and knowledge.

2 Background

Irish used to be the lingua franca in Ireland many centuries ago, but this is no longer the case. However, the vast majority of school students in Ireland study Irish for 13 years (Murtagh, 2003) in both primary and secondary school. There are several challenges to the teaching of Irish, including attitude, potential pedagogical difficulties and lack of suitable resources (including computer-based resources). This section looks at the place of Irish in the primary school system in Ireland, the problem of lack of suitable, high-quality, reliable resources for Irish for learners in general and especially for primary school children. It also looks at the role of Natural Language Processing (NLP) and Computer Assisted Language Learning (CALL) in the teaching and learning of Irish.

2.1 Irish

Irish is a morphologically-rich language that was the lingua-franca of the majority of people in Ireland until around the 17th century. Its use started to decline around this time and today there are approximately 20,000 active speakers (Ó hÉallaithe, 2004). Irish has had a complex, paradoxical socio-cultural role in Ireland. On the one hand, people in Ireland appreciate the importance of having a national language that is distinct to Ireland and understand its cultural role (DCRGA, 2009). However, they are somewhat ambivalent about its role in the education system.

2.2 Education

There are several pedagogical issues with the teaching of Irish in schools in Ireland. It is one of the core subjects and is taught on a daily basis. Often there is a lack of interest on the part of the students and their parents. Reasons such as 'it's a useless language, no one speaks it anymore', or 'why don't they teach French/Chinese instead?' are sometimes heard. Some students find it difficult. Eleven of the most commonly used verbs are highly irregular, which can be daunting and confusing for young learners. There is also the issue with lack of resources. Obviously, there is no large international market for Irish language primary school text books and publishers only have the internal market in Ireland. This limits the financial incentive for publishers to provide materials for students. In many primary schools, students have to pay for their own books, with some schools operating book rental schemes. This means that for any schools there is little or no incentive to change the books series that they use for teaching Irish. Furthermore, given the non-positive attitude some parents have towards the time/effort devoted to teaching and learning Irish in primary school, they are often not receptive to moving to a different book series if they do not have the option to buy pre-owned books for older children in the school. Harris and Murtagh (1999) and Hickey and Stenson (2010) provide a good overview of the Irish education field.

2.3 Lack of Suitable Resources

One possible strategy to incorporate a more modern approach is to use electronic resources. However, many of the resources available are not particularly suitable for primary schools students, as they are aimed at adults or may not be very accurate. Adults may be able to comprehend that the information that they see online may not be totally correct, but primary school students are not accustomed to this, as they expect the information to be correct all the time. For example, an adult may understand that "The President has super powers" or "London is the capital of Ireland" may not be true, but a child may just accept it as fact.

2.4 NLP, Computer Assisted Language Learning and Irish

Computer Assisted Language Learning (CALL) can help in the language learning process. It can help with learner motivation (e.g. Murphy and Hurd, 2011) and provide a degree of privacy for students. It enables students to repeat exercises and revise as often as they like – the computer will not tire of providing feedback to students (unlike, perhaps, a teacher in a classroom setting). Students can work at their own pace when using CALL resources – something which can be helpful in a mixed-ability class. CALL can be useful when there is limited or no access to a teacher e.g. in a minority or endangered language scenario. CALL can perhaps enhance the prestige of a minority language, by demonstrating that the language as an electronic and/or online presence. All these potential benefits can accrue to CALL for Irish. The problem is that there are several issues which hinder the development and deployment of CALL resources for Irish. From a CALL resource development point of view, the teachers may not have the time, knowledge or the expertise to develop CALL materials. There may not be the computing resources for the students to have access to the CALL materials. These factors pertain for Irish in the primary school context. The teachers cover all primary school subjects and, in general, are not trained linguists or Irish language specialists. Furthermore, while they may have reasonable computing skill, they may not have the skills and knowledge necessary required to develop Irish CALL materials. In many primary schools in Ireland, there may not be a computer in the classroom and so the students have to use a computer lab. Often, the computers are relatively old and are of a low specification, and the students have limited access to the lab. In their weekly computer slot, the teacher has to decide to use the time for English, mathematics or other school subjects.

Many CALL resources do not use any NLP e.g. the BBC Languages (World Service English) (BBC, 2014) is a general CALL resource for English language learners. Intelligent CALL (ICALL) mainly draws on Natural Language Processing (NLP) and Intelligent Tutoring Systems (ITS) (Matthews, 1993). NLP technologies can be used in CALL resources for concordancing, morphological processing and syntactic processing (Nerbonne, 2003). There are many reasons why NLP technologies are not widely used in CALL. NLP is inherently difficult and there are difficulties in integrating NLP in CALL resources. NLP researchers and NLP research is not CALL-based and there are difficulties in visualising how NLP can be used in CALL resources. Furthermore, there is a lack of knowledge amongst CALL practitioners about NLP, as the use of NLP in CALL has been driven by NLP specialists rather than CALL practitioners. Another difficulty is that NLP tools and techniques are often designed to work with correct input (Vandeventer Faltin, 2003) and language learners produce incorrect input. Also, some NLP CALL projects concentrate on the functionality/content and neglect the User Interface (UI) and this makes it difficult for the non-expert user to use the resources. However, there is a growing interest in NLP resources for language learners, particularly in the area of error detection (Leacock et al., 2014). There have been some successful NLP CALL programs (e.g. ALICE-chan (Levin and Evans, 1995)), but there are not many good examples that demonstrate the ability of NLP in CALL. Many NLP/CALL projects finish at the prototype stage and progress no further. The issue of using NLP in CALL without a good pedagogical basis must also be noted. There are also some socio-cultural factors that must also be considered including the attitudes of teachers, learners and NLP researchers to the NLP/CALL field. There are very few NLP resources available for Irish. However, two of these resources, the IFSTE and *Gramadóir*, are robust and informative and can be used in CALL resources for Irish and these are discussed below.

3 Resources

3.1 Approach

As outlined above, there is a problem with the lack of suitable, high quality CALL resources for Irish. One potential solution to this problem is to use existing NLP resources for Irish in CALL resources for the language. There are not too many such resources available for Irish, but two very useful resources are *Gramadóir* (Scannell, 2005) and the Irish Finite State Transducer Morphology Engine (Uí Dhonnchadha, 2002) (henceforth, IFSTME). These are both high-quality, reliable and accurate resources that are publicly available. These resources were integrated into two Irish CALL resources for primary school children. *Gramadóir* was used in a Writing Checker Component (WCC) and the IFSTME was used in a Verb Conjugation Component (VCC). The overall architecture ran on an Apache server, with static pages stored in the `htdocs` directory and dynamic pages stored in the `cgi-bin` directory. XML technologies and Perl were core components of the CALL software.

3.2 Verb Conjugation Component

Uí Dhonnchadh's (2002) Irish Finite State Transducer Morphology Engine (IFSTME) is a comprehensive resource which supplies morphological information for Irish words and sentences. The IFSTME was used to generate the verb conjugations for verbs in the past simple tense.

The aim of the Verb Conjugation Component (VCC) is to provide a tool to produce static and animated verb conjugation web pages based on externally supplied verb data. The underlying engine is an Irish Finite State Transducer Morphology Engine (IFSTME) (Uí Dhonnchadha, 2002). It was combined with an animation tool (Koller, 2004) and a CALL Template (Ward, 2001) to provide an Irish verb learning tool for primary school students. Figure 1 shows the information flow for the VCC. The external source of verb information (i.e. the IFSTME) provides information on verbs to the VCC which uses the information in the CALL resources.

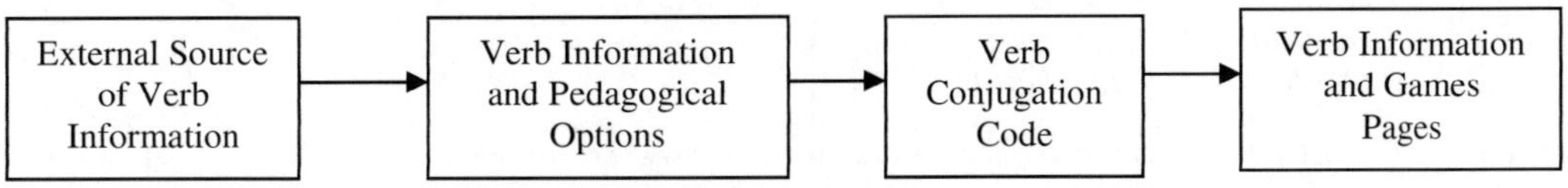

Figure 1 Information Flow for the Verb Conjugation Component

Figure 2 shows an overview of the VCC. The external verb information (from the IFSTME) is combined with local code files and local configuration files in the VCC. The teacher provided pedagogical input to the process. The VCC combines this data with flash animation code to produce verb information files, activity files and report files for the learner to use. The teacher can also see the report files.

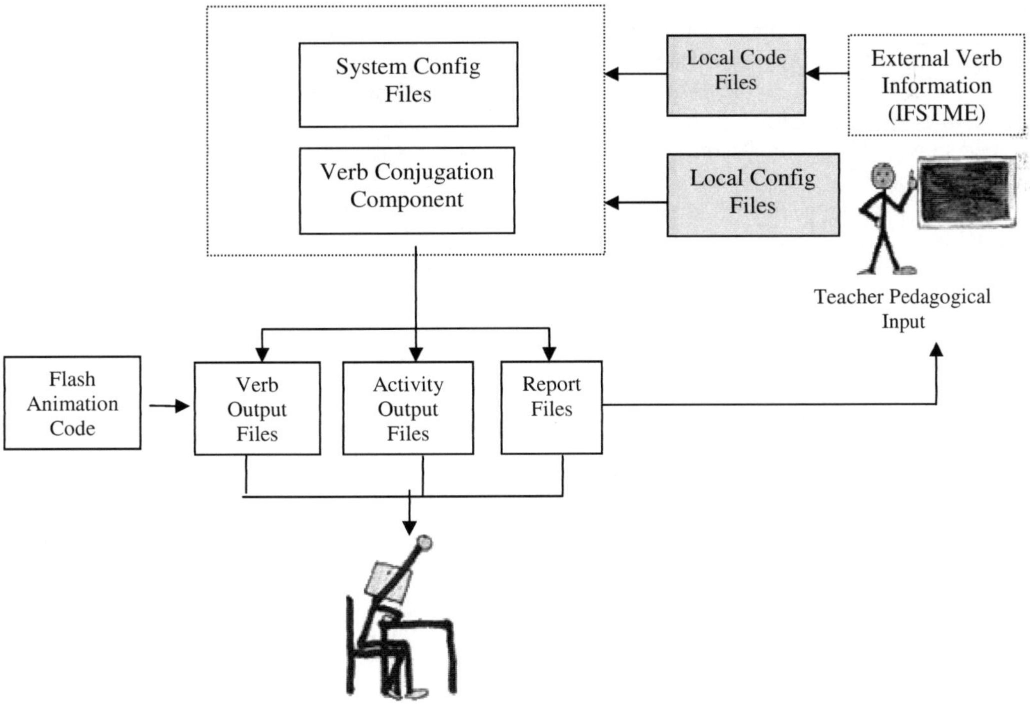

Figure 2: Overview of the VCC

The IFSTME provides an analyser and generator for Irish inflectional morphology for nouns, adjectives and verbs. Replace rule triggers (for stems and affixes) are combined with replace rules written as regular expressions (for word mutations) to produce a two-level morphological transducer for Irish. The VCC only uses a very small subset of the verb forms provided by the IME (there are 52 forms in all). It has web pages for 20 verbs, in both static and dynamic forms. Figure 3 shows the past indicative information for *bris* (to break) supplied by the Irish Finite State Morphology Engine (Uí Dhonnchadha, 2002). Note that the output is not intended to be used as presented by the end-user, hence the presence of ^FH and ^FS tags in Figure 3. Figure 4 shows the animated verb page for *bris* (past tense).

Bris+Verb+PastInd	b^FHris
Bris+Verb+PastInd+1P+Pl	b^FHris^FSeamar
Bris+Verb+PastInd+Auto	bris^FSeadh
Bris+Verb+PastInd+Auto+Neg	bris^FSeadh
Bris+Verb+PastInd+Auto+NegQ	bris^FSeadh
Bris+Verb+PastInd+Auto+Q	bris^FSeadh

Figure 3: Past Indicative Information for *bris* (to break)

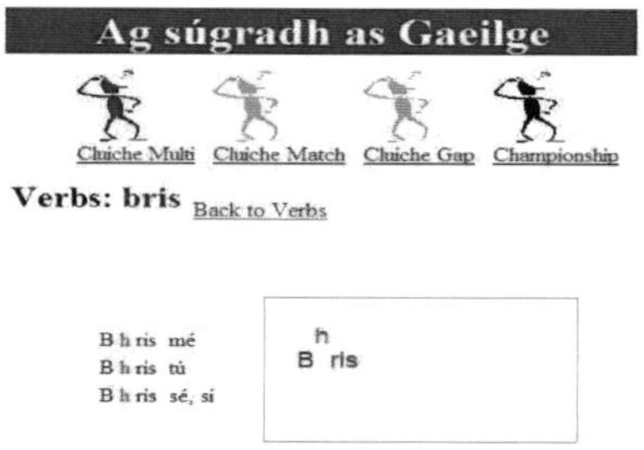

Figure 4: Animated Verb Page for *bris*

3.3 Writing Checker Component

The Writing Checker Component (WCC) provides a tool that checks the learner's text input and provides feedback on spelling and grammar errors. It adapts an externally supplied grammar checker, *Gramadóir* (Scannell, 2005) to the needs of primary school students. *Gramadóir* is an open source grammar checker that has been implemented for Irish and it can be used on a variety of operating systems. It is modular in design and provides separate components for sentence segmentation, spell checking, part-of-speech tagging and grammar checking. It is easy to use and there is a simple command line interface and a web interface to the software. It is corpus-based and is booted from web-based corpora. It is easy to port to other languages as the language developers' pack provided is designed so that no programming experience is required. It is scalable. Spell checking packages can be developed in a few hours, while the engine also accommodates the development of a full-scale grammar checker.

Gramadóir is an excellent, accurate Irish language resource. It is aimed at linguistically-aware adults. It can be used in white-box mode and be adapted to the needs of the users. However, a black-box approach was taken when developing a writing checker for primary school students. Under this approach, the grammar error messages to the user were passed through a filter and substituted with more suitable error messages for the target learners.

There was an initial pilot study to test the feasibility of the resources and there were several design modifications based on learner and teacher feedback. For example, there was a need to convert the adult learner-oriented language of *Gramadóir*'s errors messages to language more appropriate to younger learners. Some of the original *Gramadóir*'s error messages and their WCC equivalent are shown in Table 1. Note that not all students would understand the words "*urú*" and "*séimhiú*" even thought the teacher may have explained them.

There was a need to separate out spelling errors from grammar errors and an error classification file was used to classify *Gramadóir*'s errors as either grammar or spelling errors. Sometimes, *Gramadóir* failed to suggest any alternatives for spelling errors and the Levenshtein algorithm (implemented with code from Merriampark (2005)) was used to check suitable words from the local dictionary. The local dictionary consisted of words from the some class texts. A word with a Levenshtien value of 1 was probably the word the student intended to use, while those with a value of 2 were probably suitable. There was also a need to be able to correct and resubmit a text. The screen layout had to be changed so that more information could be viewed at once and to minimise scrolling. A review of the errors detected and not detected by *Gramdóir* was required and certain adaptations were necessary.

Gramadóir Message	Writing Checker Message
	Humm, there might be an error here
Definite article required	'an' required
Eclipsis missing	You need a letter at the start of the word
Lenition missing	You might be missing a 'h' here
Prefix \d'\ missing	You need a 'd' here
The dependent form of the verb …	The verb is not correct
The genitive case	You need to add something here

Table 1. *Gramadóir* Error Messages and their WCC Equivalent

Table 2 shows some sample student text, along with some of the error types and the changes made to *Gramadóir*'s error messages. Note that the missing word "*seomra*" before "*suite*" was not detected in example 3 in Table 2.

Error Type	Text	*Gramadóir* Error Message	Expected Error	New Error Message
Gramadóir error OK	Tá bosca beag agam ach tá níos bosca lú agat..	Usually used in the set phrase /níos lú, is lú/	As expected	Usually used in the set phrase /níos lú, is lú/
Gramadóir error OK, but msg not suitable	Tá trí gloine atá an mbord.	Unnecessary eclipsis	As expected	Maybe you should have **ar an mbord**
Error detected, but should be ignored	Shuigh Ciara agus Maire sa suite ar an tolg.	It seems unlikely that you intended to use the subjunctive here (Maire)		
Error incorrectly detected	Fuair **Ríona** páipéar.	Unnecessary use of the genitive case		
Unreported error	Shuil Eoin isteach seomra folctha.			Maybe you should have **sa** after the word **isteach**

Table 2. Error Types and WCC Changes

Table 3 shows some sample learner text and some of the key error phrases used for spelling errors. The fact that neither *Gramadóir* nor the WCC was able to detect the word 'picture' is interesting, as it shows that they do not handle code-mixing, which would be quite common amongst primary school learners. This could be an area of future interest.

Error Phrases	Example	Source	*Gramadóir*	WCC
Do you mean	Nior tharraing sé	Learner	Do you mean /níor/ ?	**Níor**
Unknown word	Torraing	Learner	Unknown word	**???**
Not in database	Picture	Learner	Not in databasc but may be a compound /pic+túr/?	**???**

Table 3 Key Error Phrases for Spelling Errors

The overall logic for the WCC is shown in Figure 5.

Use the local error checking routines)
Read and process learner text
Depending on configuration options ….
- If External error checking on … check for external errors
- if local error check on … check for local errors
Display user text with grammar and spelling messages (if any)

Figure 5. Overall Logic for the WCC

A sample of student text in the WCC is shown in Figure 6.

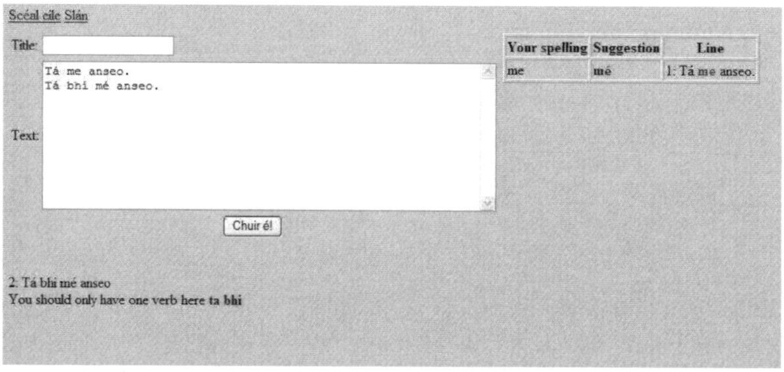

Figure 6. Sample of Student Text in WCC

4 Deployment and Evaluation

4.1 Deployment

The VCC and the WCC were used by primary schools students in two English-medium schools in Ireland. One of the schools was a mainstream, standard school (School 1) and the other was a school in a disadvantaged area (School 2). Ethical approval was applied for and obtained from the University's Research Ethics Committee and the parents. 3rd (age 8 – 9) and 4th class students (age 9 - 10) from School 1 used the VCC and 4th class students from School 2 used the WCC. The students used the resources over a period of several months on an ad-hoc basis.

4.2 Evaluation

Evaluation in the CALL field is complex. Quantitative and qualitative evaluation and formative and summative evaluation are all important. The VCC and WCC were evaluated using several different criteria. The aim of using various different evaluation criteria was to try to evaluate the Irish CALL resources from different perspectives. Chapelle's (2001) and Colpaert's (2004) CALL evaluation criteria were used to evaluate the VCC and WCC as CALL artefacts. The ICT4LT (2005) website which provides a CALL software evaluation checklist, was also used. The limitations of the evaluations include that some of it is based on self-reporting by young learners and that it was a small scale study with irregular and uneven usage.

The VCC was evaluated by the teacher and students in the mainstream school. An anonymous questionnaire-based survey was completed by 20 students (6 students were missing on the day of the questionnaire). There were both open and closed questions and students were encouraged to provide (negative) feedback. With regards to the VCC, the students 40% liked the tool, 45% liked it a little and only 15% did not like it. The majority found it helpful (45%) or a little helpful (35%), with only 20% saying it was not helpful. The majority preferred the animate mode (60%), over the static mode (15%), with 10% slightly preferring the animated mode, while 15% did not see the animated pages. The teacher found the resource useful as it was aligned with her teaching objectives for the class. Table 4 shows a summary of the student feedback on the VCC.

Question	Yes	No	A little/Both	Didn't see
Did you like the verb lessons?	40%	15%	45%	
Did you find them helpful?	45%	20%	35%	
Do you prefer the animated mode?	60%	15%	10%	15%

Table 4. Student Feedback on the Verb Conjugation Component

Students were also asked to give feedback after doing exercises/games with the VCC. The total number of students who answered online was 22 (note that not all students answered all the questions). Most students (84%) reported that they found the verb pages at least somewhat helpful, with little difference between those who viewed the pages in static and animated modes. It is interesting to note that more static mode students (26%) than animated mode students (10%) found the exercise/game hard. Table 5 shows a summary of the online student feedback data on the VCC.

Question	No	A Little	Yes
Did you find the verb lessons helpful?	16%	35%	49%
Static:	17%	35%	48%
Animated:		35%	50%
Did you like the end of lesson games?	12%	19%	70%
Static:	13%	13%	65%
Animated:	10%	25%	74%
Did you find the end of lesson games hard?	46%	36%	18%
Static:	35%	39%	26%
Animated:	57%	33%	10%

Table 5. Student Online Feedback on the Verb Conjugation Component

Students who did not find the VCC helpful said that they know the verbs already or that it was boring. Those who found it helpful said it "shows and tell what it means" and another reported that it cleared up confusion ("I was always getting confused and now I'm not"). When asked about their preference between static and animated mode, students who preferred static mode said that they understand it when the teacher explains it or that they found the animation mode annoying. Those who liked the animated mode said it was more enjoyable and it helped them. A summary of students' comments about the VCC are shown in Table 6. Note that the comments are provided as written by the students.

Did you find the Verb part helpful? **No:** Know already Too boring	**Did you find the Verb part helpful?** **Yes:** Shows and tells what it means Tells you how to spell them and more I was always getting confused and now I'm not
Which mode do you prefer? **Static:** I get it when the teacher tells me It's annoying	**Which mode do you prefer?** **Animated:** You would know more past tense verbs More fun Makes me understand It helps I kept on forgetting the h It will get you used to putting in silent letters
What was the best part and why? Games: learn stuff in games, fun	**What was the least enjoyable part and why?** Some games too part (paraphrased)

Table 6. Students' Comments on the Verb Conjugation Component

The teacher also provided an evaluation of the VCC. She said that it had sufficient learning potential because it focused on verb conjugation forms and her students did well in the verb exercises. She thought it was suitable for the learners, it was sufficiently challenging for them, it had the right level of difficulty and that the tasks were appropriate for them. The teacher said that explicit exposure to verb conjugation forms was pedagogically appropriate for her students. Note that another teacher was also involved in using and evaluating the VCC, but for external reasons was not able to use the resource to any great extent and the findings from her class are excluded from the evaluation.

Students in both schools used the WCC, but the findings here relate to the students in the mainstream school, as the numbers who used the WCC in the disadvantaged school were limited. The learners were asked to provide their feedback on the WCC via an anonymous open and closed questionnaire. Nineteen students completed the survey (7 students were absent on the day of the survey). Students reported that they liked using the WCC (yes (20%) and a little (50%), but 28% did not like it and a minority (28%) did not find it helpful. A sizeable minority reported that they did not understand the grammar error messages (42%) and spelling error messages (32%) and therefore, not surprisingly, many (grammar 47%, spelling 30%) said that they did not find them helpful. Most students said that they corrected their grammar errors (75%) and spelling errors (59%), although the empirical data does confirm this. It must be noted that only 11% said they liked writing in Irish and a majority (63%) said they would prefer to write in their copy than use the WCC. Table 7 provides a summary of the student feedback on the WCC.

Question	Yes	A Little	No
Did you like using the WCC?	22%	50%	28%
Did you find the WCC helpful?	44%	28%	28%
Did you understand the grammar error messages?	16%	42%	42%
Did you understand the spelling error messages?	26%	42%	32%
Did you find the grammar error messages helpful?	29%	24%	47%
Did you find the spelling error messages helpful?	35%	35%	30%
Did you correct your grammar errors?	75%		25%
Did you correct your spelling errors?	59%		41%
Do you like writing in Irish?	11%	47%	42%
Would you prefer to write in your copy?	63%		37%

Table 7. Student Feedback on the Writing Checker Component

Some of the reasons given for not finding it helpful included: "it was boring/hard", "I already know how to write" or "I don't like writing". Those who thought it was helpful said it told them the errors in their texts. Table 8 shows some of the students' comments on the WCC. Note the comments are paraphrased, based on comments provided by the students.

Question	Finding
Why do you like/dislike writing in Irish?	Like: It's our national language Dislike: Hard, boring, hard spellings, accents
Would you prefer the WCC or your copy for writing?	WCC: tells you your mistakes Copy: easier, faster, no keyboard problems

Table 8. Student Comments on the Writing Checker Component

The mainstream school teacher also completed a questionnaire and the feedback was positive. The teacher said that the WCC was beneficial for the students and enabled the students to construct sentences and stories. She felt that it was at an appropriate level for the learners as all the students could use the software. She said that it helped to consolidate classroom work. She said the main problem was that she did not know enough about computers herself. The teacher in the disadvantaged school initially came up with the idea to distinguish between grammar and spelling errors, as spelling errors were not a priority for her. There were logistical difficulties for the teacher in that only four students (out of 17) were considered sufficiently competent to use and benefit from the WCC. Another difficulty was the fact that the school computer lab was closed during the project academic year and students had to travel to another venue to actually use the WCC – this obviously is not ideal.

Although both schools were boys-only schools in the same city, there are some significant differences between them. In the mainstream school, the students use the recommended textbook for their class, while in the disadvantaged school the students use a textbook for a more junior year. Also, more students are exempt from studying Irish in the disadvantaged school and there are fewer above-average students. Classroom management is more difficult and there are students leaving and returning to class from attending sessions with special needs teachers. This highlights the need to have flexible resources that can be used as the teacher sees fit. While the teacher in the disadvantaged school appreciated what the CALL resources can provide, their usage would probably be on a more ad-hoc basis than in the mainstream school.

From a CALL development point of view, it was relatively straightforward to use both Irish NLP tools. The IFSTME provides comprehensive information on Irish verbs. For pedagogical reasons, the VCC only uses a small subset of the information. The students were learning only a limited set of verbs, mainly regular verbs and some important irregular ones. In theory, the VCC could be modified easily to incorporate a more complete list of verbs, persons and tenses (although this was not required for this group of students). There were some difficulties in mapping and interpreting the conjugation changes for irregular verbs, but it must be noted that the IFSTME was not intended as a verb conjugation mechanism. It was used in white-box mode (i.e. some internal knowledge of the software was required for the VCC), but overall it was worthwhile using the IFSTME. Likewise, *Gramadóir* was a useful NLP resource for developing the WCC. It was robust and reliable and it would not have been possible to build the WCC without it.

5 Discussion

The VCC and the WCC demonstrate that it is possible and feasible to develop pedagogical, targeted NLP CALL resources for Irish. It helped that the two NLP tools used were robust and of a high quality. The learners and teachers were unaware of the underlying technology (and this is desirable). However, as is often the case, the problems were logistical rather than technical (Egbert et al., 2002; Ward, 2007). Access to computers and "space in the timetable" hindered the continued deployment of the Irish CALL resources.

It is important for NLP researchers working with any language to disseminate their findings and make their resources available to people outside the NLP community. It is even more important for NLP researchers working with minority languages to do so, as the resources are usually limited (Woodbury, 2003; Lam et al., 2014) and the pool of people working with the language small. Speakers, learners and other interested parties of minority languages are used to trying to do a lot with a little, and making NLP resources available to them could lead to the development of resources not initially envisioned by the NLP researchers.

6 Conclusion

This paper reports on how two NLP resources for Irish (i.e. the IFSTME and *Gramadóir*) were used to develop CALL resources for primary school children learning Irish. It shows that these NLP resources for Irish can be adapted and used to develop appropriate CALL resources. In order for the CALL materials to be successful, it is important that there is a seamless integration of the NLP tools in the CALL resources, so that the learner is unaware of their existence. Suitable, robust and accurate NLP resources are required, if the CALL materials are to work in a real deployment situation. The CALL resource should not fail or be inaccurate. The integration of the CALL resources with the curriculum itself is key if the resources are actually going to be used by the teacher and the students (Bull and Zakrzewski, 1997, Mc Carthy, 1999; Ward, 2007). This applies regardless of the language being studied – if the CALL resources do not help the teacher and aligned with the curriculum, they will not be used. There are other, non-technical, non-NLP related factors that help or hinder the actual usage of CALL resources. It should be noted that in order for the NLP resources to be used in the first place, there needs to be an awareness of their existence - teachers and CALL developers must know that relevant NLP resources are available. This places an onus on NLP researchers to disseminate their research and tools to a wider audience than perhaps they would normally address. They could interact with the CALL community via CALL conferences and especially with ICALL (Intelligent-CALL) researchers via their Special Interest Groups (SIGs), conferences and workshops. This is particularly pertinent in the minority and endangered language context (e.g. Irish and other Celtic languages), where technical, financial and researcher resources are limited.

References

BBC. 2014. *BBC Languages (World Service English).* Available at: http://www.bbc.co.uk/worldservice/learningenglish/

Joanna Bull and Stan Zakrzewski. 1997. Implementing learning technologies: a university-wide approach. *Active Learning, 6*, 15-19.

Carol Chapelle. 2001. *Computer applications in second language acquisition: Foundations for teaching testing and research.* Cambridge: CUP

Jozef Colpaert. 2004. *Design of online interactive language courseware: conceptualization, specification and prototyping: research into the impact of linguistic-didactic functionality on software architecture.*- Antwerpen: Universiteit Antwerpen, Faculteit Letteren en Wijsbegeerte, Departement Taalkunde, 2004 - Doctoral dissertation

DCRGA. 2009. *20-year strategy for the Irish Language.* Prepared for the Department of Community, Rural and Gaeltacht Affairs. Fiontar, Dublin City University.

Joy Egbert,, Trena M. Paulus and Yoko Nakamichi. 2002. The impact of CALL instruction on classroom computer use: A foundation for rethinking technology in teacher education. *Language Learning & Technology, 6*(3), 108-126.

John Harris and Lelia Murtagh. 1999. *Teaching and Learning Irish in Primary School.* Dublin: ITÉ.

Tina Hickey and Nancy Stenson.. 2011. Irish orthography: what do teachers and learners need to know about it, and why?. *Language, Culture and Curriculum,24*(1).

Thomas Koller. 2004. Creation and evaluation of animated grammars. Eurocall 2004, Vienna, Austria (3rd September 2004).

ICT4LT. 2005. *Information and Communications Technology for Language Teaching (ICT4LT) Project: Evaluation Forms*

Lori S. Levin and David A. Evans. 1995. ALICE-cha: A Case Study in ICALL Theory and Practice. *In*: V. M. Holland, J.D. Kaplan and M.R. Sams (Eds.) *Intelligent Language Tutors* (pp. 327-44). Mahwah: Lawrence Erlbaum

Khang N. Lam, Feras Al Tarouti and Jugal Kalita. 2014. Creating Lexical Resources for Endangered Languages. *ComputEL at ACL 2014.*

Claudia Leacock., Martin Chodorow, Michael Gamon and Joel Tetreault. 2014. Automated grammatical error detection for language learners. *Synthesis lectures on human language technologies.* Second Edition.

C. Matthews. 1993. Grammar frameworks in Intelligent CALL. *CALICO Journal* 11, 1: 5-27.

Brian McCarthy. 1999. Integration: the sine qua non of CALL. *CALL-EJ Online,1*(2), 1-12.

Merriampark. 2005. *Levenshtein distance algorithm.*

Linda Murphy and Stella Hurd. 2011. Fostering learner autonomy and motivation in blended teaching. In: Nicolson, Margaret; Murphy, Linda and Southgate, Margaret eds. *Language Teaching in Blended Contexts.*Edinburgh, U.K.: Dunedin Academic Press Ltd, pp. 43–56.

Lelia Murtagh. 2003. *Retention and Attrition of Irish as a Second Language: a longitudinal study of general and communicative proficiency in Irish among second level school leavers and the influence of instructional background, language use and attitude/motivation variables.* PhD thesis, University of Groningen.

John Nerbonne. 2003. Natural Language Processing in Computer-Aided Language Learning. *In:* S. Mitkov (Ed.) *The Oxford Handbook of Computational Linguistics.* Oxford: OUP

Donncha Ó hÉallaithe. 2004. From Language Revival to Survival. In: C. M. Murchaidh (ed.), *Who Needs Irish? Reflections on the Importance of the Irish Language Today*, Dublin: Veritas Publications.

Pádraig Ó Riagáin. and M. Ó Gliasáin. 1994. National Survey on Languages 1993: Preliminary Report. *Dublin: Institiuid Teangeolaiochta Eireann.*

Kevin Scannell. 2005. *An Gramadóir.* Available at: http://borel.slu.edu/gramadoir/

Thornbury H., Elder M., Crowe D., Bennett P. & Belton V. 1996. Suggestions for successful integration. *Active Learning*, 4, 18-23.

Elaine Uí Dhonnchadha. 2002. Two-level Finite-State Morphology for Irish, *In: Proceedings of LREC 2002 3 rd International Conference on Language resources and Evaluation.* Las Palmas de Gran Canaria, Spain.

Anne Vandeventer Faltin. 2003. *Syntactic Error Diagnosis in the context of Computer Assisted Language Learning.* PhD Thesis, Faculté des letters d l'Université de Genève.

Monica Ward. 2001. *A Template for CALL Programs for Endangered Languages.* Masters thesis Dublin City University.

Monica Ward. 2007. *A template for CALL programs for endangered languages.* (Doctoral dissertation, Dublin City University).

Tony Woodbury. 2003. Defining documentary linguistics. *Language documentation and description, 1*(1), 35-51.

Tools facilitating better use of online dictionaries: Technical aspects of Multidict, Wordlink and Clilstore

Caoimhín P. Ó Donnaíle
Sabhal Mòr Ostaig
An t-Eilean Sgitheanach
IV44 8RQ, UK
caoimhin@smo.uhi.ac.uk

Abstract

The Internet contains a plethora of openly available dictionaries of many kinds, translating between thousands of language pairs. Three tools are described, Multidict, Wordlink and Clilstore, all openly available at multidict.net, which enable these diverse resources to be harnessed, unified, and utilised in ergonomic fashion. They are of particular benefit to intermediate level language learners, but also to researchers and learners of all kinds. Multidict facilitates finding and using online dictionaries in hundreds of languages, and enables easy switching between different dictionaries and target languages. It enables the utilization of page-image dictionaries in the Web Archive. Wordlink can link most webpages word by word to online dictionaries via Multidict. Clilstore is an open store of language teaching materials utilizing the power of Wordlink and Multidict. The programing and database structures and ideas behind Multidict, Wordlink and Clilstore are described.

1 Introduction

At `multidict.net` three tools are to be found, Multidict, Wordlink and Clilstore. Their development was funded by EC projects with the aim of developing and sharing tools for language learning, and thanks to this they are a freely and openly available resource. They support not only the major European languages, but also place a particular emphasis on supporting minority languages including the Celtic languages. They also currently support scores of non-European languages and have the potential to support many more.

The central idea behind them is that one of the best ways of learning a language is to use authentic materials as early as possible - materials which are of interest for their own sake. This is the "**CLIL**", "Content and Language Integrated Learning", in the name "Clilstore". In the past, this would have meant either the students laboriously looking up word after word in the dictionary, or else the teacher laboriously preparing glossaries of the most difficult words for each piece of reading material. Good authentic content is easy to find via the Internet for most subjects in most languages, but preparing the glossaries was tedious.

For the students, online dictionaries, and there are many of them, sped up the process of looking up words compared to the old paper dictionaries. But it was still tedious typing in words, and then typing or copying them in again to try them in another dictionary. Far better if you could just click on a word in a text to look it up. This is the idea behind **Wordlink**. It takes any webpage and modifies the html so that every word is linked to online dictionaries while the presentation of the page remains the same.

Proceedings of the First Celtic Language Technology Workshop, pages 18–27,
Dublin, Ireland, August 23 2014.

Automatic glossing of text as an aid to learners is not an idea unique to this project. It is used by the Rikaichan[1] Firefox add-on for Japanese, by the BBC Vocab[2] facility for Welsh and Gaelic, by the Readlang[3] website, by the PIE[4] Chrome add-on for English, and by many e-books. While these systems have many advantages, they also have severe restrictions compared to Wordlink: restrictions to particular languages, or particular browsers, or particular websites, or particular in-house dictionaries. Wordlink differs in that it attempts to generalize to very many languages and to harness the many freely available online dictionaries.

The earliest versions of Wordlink contained the code and knowledge required to link to a range of online dictionaries translating to various target languages. But the list quickly became ridiculously long and it was realized that the work of selecting and accessing different dictionaries needed to be hived off to a separate facility. So **Multidict** was created, and is a tremendously useful standalone facility in its own right.

Finally **Clilstore** was created to make it easy for language teachers to create materials and lessons utilizing the power of Wordlink and Multidict, and to make it easy for students and teachers to find material of interest stored openly in Clilstore. The great thing about Clilstore is that it enables students to access interesting material which would otherwise be a bit too difficult for them to cope with. It has proved to be particularly useful to intermediate level learners, and to learners coming from cognate languages.

We now look at the technical workings behind each of these three tools in turn.

2 Multidict

2.1 The interface

Here is what Multidict looks like in use:

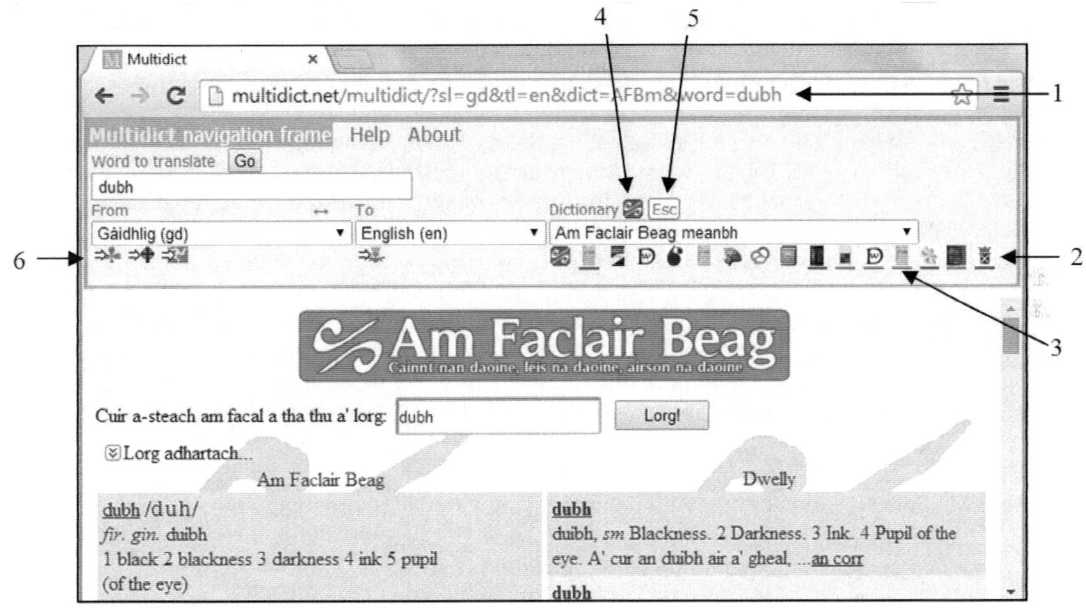

Figure 1. The Multidict interface

The section at the top is the "Multidict navigation frame" which controls dictionary selection and lookup. (Yes, Multidict uses old-fashioned frames[5].) Below that is the frame containing the output returned by the online dictionary. In this case Multidict is being used to look up the Gàidhlig word

---

[1] http://rikaichan.mozdev.org (this and all web references are as accessed on the date of writing, 2014-06-24)
[2] http://www.bbc.co.uk/cymru/vocab/
[3] http://www.learngaelic.net/advanced/lganla/index.jsp?lang=gd
[4] https://sites.google.com/site/phoneticallyintuitiveenglish/using-pie/getting-a-word-s-meaning
[5] http://www.w3.org/TR/html401/present/frames.html
http://www.w3.org/TR/html5/obsolete.html

dubh in the Gàidhlig to English dictionary *Am Faclar Beag meanbh*[6] (the concise version of *Am Faclair Beag*[7]).

Note (**1**) the url which can be used to refer to the dictionary output for this word. This can be particularly useful in the case of dictionaries which do not themselves have any way of linking to their output via a url. The "sl" stands for "source language" and "tl" stands for "target language".

Note (**2**) the row of 16x16 pixel **favicons** for dictionaries. Clicking on one of these switches you to the corresponding dictionary. They give the navigation frame a cluttered appearance, but once you get to know them they are much quicker and more convenient than selecting a dictionary using the dropdown selector. If the dictionary website has its own favicon, as most do, then Multidict uses that. If not, we try to construct a mnemonic favicon for the dictionary using the dictionary's own colours. Both in the row of favicons and in the dictionary dropdown, the dictionaries are placed in some kind of compromise order of preference. Note (**3**) that some favicons have an underline. This signals that the dictionary is a **page-image** dictionary where the user will have to scan around by eye on the page to find the word in question. More about page-image dictionaries in section 2.7 below. An overline where present above a favicon signals that the dictionary is a concise version, perhaps designed for mobile phones, which can often be very useful if the dictionary is being used together with Wordlink.

Note (**4**) the favicon for the current dictionary, and (**5**) the **Esc** button which provides a convenient way of escape from Multidict's frames to the dictionary's own homepage. Multidict is in fact a very convenient way of finding dictionaries and we have no desire to keep users on Multidict if they prefer to head off and use the dictionary directly.

Multidict does not itself have any dictionary information, but relies entirely on directing users to online dictionaries. So we need to be fair and maintain **good relations with dictionary owners**. Multidict makes a point of never "scraping"[8], never even caching information from dictionary pages. Output is always presented exactly as it comes from the dictionary, complete with any advertising. In fact, whenever possible, Multidict operates by sending a simple HTTP "redirect" to redirect the user's browser to the dictionary page. Multidict advertises to dictionary owners that they can ask for their dictionary to be removed from Multidict's database at any time for any reason, but no dictionary owner has ever requested this.

Note (**6**) the "favicon" symbols for switching to **closely related languages**. This makes it easy, for example, to switch and look for the word *dubh* in Irish dictionaries instead of Scottish Gaelic. For most languages we just use language codes for these symbols, but for the Celtic languages we have colourful symbols available. The same is possible for the target language, although in the example above the only symbol shown is the "Gàidhlig" symbol for switching to Gàidhlig-Gàidhlig monolingual dictionaries. To support this system, the Multidict database has two tables holding information on closely related languages. Two tables because "closely related" for the purposes of the target language field may not be the same as closely related for the purposes of the source language field. There would be no point in trying an "sr-Latn" (Serbian in Latin script) word in an "sr" (Serbian in Cyrillic script) dictionary, but someone who understood "sr" could be expected to understand "sr-Latn".

2.2 The database behind it

How does Multidict work? For many dictionaries, very very simply. If when you look up the word *dubh* at `friendlydict.org`, you notice that the url is

`http://friendlydict.org/find?facail=dubh`

then you can be sure that by simply replacing `dubh` with `geal` in the url, you would look up the word *geal*. For such dictionaries, the Multidict database would store the string

`http://friendlydic.org/find?facail={word}`

and when the time came to look up a word, Multidict would simply replace `{word}` with the word in question and redirect the results frame to this address.

However, for many dictionaries, both good ones and less good, things are not so simple. Their html form submission uses **POST** method instead of **GET** method and there is no sign of a nice url containing the word to search for. In this case, Multidict has to construct and send an http POST request. It

6 http://www.faclair.com/m/
7 http://www.faclair.com
8 The practice of extracting partial information from webpages on another site: http://en.wikipedia.org/wiki/Web_scraping

does this using the HTTP_Request2 PEAR[9] class. (PEAR being a repository of software for the PHP language.) Multidict captures the response to the request and despatches it to the results frame.

Multidict, Wordlink and Clilstore are written in PHP, and behind them is a mySQL (or MariaDB[10] to be precise) database. The database has a `dict` table with a record for each dictionary, storing the long name, the favicon and the dictionary's homepage address.

However, many dictionaries serve several languages, and the main business is done by the table `dictParam`, which is indexed by `(dict, sl, tl)`. This table stores the url, as described above, any post parameters required, and has many other fields. A field called `message` can contain a tip to be displayed to users in the navigation frame, such as "Right-click to zoom". A field `charextra` can specify certain different kinds of extra processing to be applied to the word before lookup to satisfy the peculiarities of particular dictionaries. Some dictionaries require accents to be stripped from the word, some require them to be urlencoded[11]. The Irish Dineen[12] dictionary requires 'h's to be stripped from the word to convert to old spelling and dictionary order, and this is indicated by the string "striph" in the `charextra` field. A field `handling` specifies any particular handling required to obtain the output from the dictionary. The best behaved dictionaries get the value "redirect". Some particularly awkward dictionaries which require POST parameters and only accept requests from the user's browser get the value "form". This causes Multidict to construct a form in the results frame, fill in the search word, and cause the user's browser via Javascript to immediately submit it. Thus Multidict has a whole range of clever tricks and tools available to it, which means that it manages to handle between 80% and 90% of all dictionaries we have attempted to link to.

2.3 Language codes

Multidict currently tries to use IETF language codes[13] both externally and internally. i.e. It uses a two-letter ISO 639-1[14] language code such as "en", "fr", "de", "ga", "gd" if such is available, or a three letter ISO 639-3[15] language code such as "sco", "sga" when no two-letter code is available, and it sometimes makes use of country code and script code extensions such as "pt-BR" and "sr-Latn". When these are inadequate, such as for historic languages and dialects, it turns to LinguistList[16] codes for inspiration: e.g. "non-swe" (Old Swedish[17]), and "oci-ara" (Aranese[18]).

Where ISO 639-3 equates a two-letter language code with a three letter code denoting a **macrolanguage**[19], as in the case of Latvian lt=lav which also includes Latgalian, Multidict uses the ISO 639-3 code for the precise language, in this case "lvs" for Standard Latvian. This differs from Google Translate, for example, which continues to use the two-letter code code for the dominant language in the macrolanguage grouping. Other languages where similar questions arise include Estonian et/ekk, Malay ms/zsm, Albanian sq/als, Azari az/azj, Uzbek uz/uzn, Persian fa/pes, Guarani gn/gug, Swahili sw/swh.

2.4 Closely related languages

As we increasingly try to cater for minority languages and dialects, the questions of how to deal with closely related languages become ever greater. On the one hand, we want to distinguish European Portuguese, currently coded as "pt", and Brazilian Portuguese, "pt-BR", especially if the dictionary site itself clearly distinguishes them among its language choices. On the other hand, we don't want users to be unable to find dictionaries which might be very useful to them, simply because of a small

---

9 http://pear.php.net/package/HTTP_Request2/
10 https://mariadb.org
11 http://www.php.net//manual/en/function.urlencode.php
12 http://glg.csisdmz.ul.ie
13 https://tools.ietf.org/html/rfc5646
14 http://en.wikipedia.org/wiki/List_of_ISO_639-1_codes
15 http://www-01.sil.org/iso639-3/
16 http://linguistlist.org/forms/langs/find-a-language-or-family.cfm
17 http://multitree.org/codes/non-swe
18 http://multitree.org/codes/oci-ara
19 http://www-01.sil.org/iso639-3/macrolanguages.asp
http://en.wikipedia.org/wiki/ISO_639_macrolanguage

difference in language code. The "closely related languages" feature in the Multidict interface goes a very small way towards addressing this difficulty, but the problem requires more thought.

A webpage[20] available via the Multidict help system lists all the languages currently handled by Multidict. It lists languages ordered by language family, then sub-family and so on. Closely related languages are therefore located close together, and the webpage can be used to maintain Multidict's tables of closely related languages. To achieve this ordering, the Multidict database links each of its language codes to the corresponding LinguistList code, and holds a copy of the LinguistList Multitree[21] Composite Tree. However, because the Composite Tree provides nothing but a tree structure, albeit a tremendously useful finely-detailed tree structure, it is in itself inadequate for defining the required linearization of the tree. We always prefer to place the most closely related branches (closely related by geography if nothing else) adjacent to one another, rather than the children of each node being listed in some random order (as they currently are in Multitree itself, which places Baltic languages next to Celtic and Armenian, rather than next to Slavic). To do this, in Multidict's copy of the Composite Tree, we maintain, where relevant to Multidict, an ordering of the children of a parent node. This has to be laboriously researched each time a language is added to Multidict. It would be very useful if this ordering information were to be provided as a resource together with the LinguistList Composite Tree.

2.5 "n×n" dictionaries

Most online dictionaries only handle a limited number of language pair `(sl, tl)` combinations, and each of these is given a separate record in the `dictParam` table. However, some online dictionaries can translate between any of n×n language pairs. Most notably in recent years, Glosbe[22] and Global Glossary[23] translate surprisingly successfully between any pair out of hundreds of languages. To harness the tremendous power of these "n×n" dictionaries without cluttering the `dictParam` table with tens of thousands of records, the Multidict database uses the following tactic. In the sl field in the `dictParam` table, a "¤" symbol is placed, and this indicates to Multidict to refer to a separate table `dictLang` to obtain a list of the n languages which this particular n×n dictionary handles. The table can also translate between the language code used by Multidict and a different language code used by the dictionary. In the `dictParam` table, the url required for linking to the dictionary can (as can also the POST parameters) contain placeholders for sl and tl, such as for example:

```
http://friendlydic.org/find?from={sl}&to={tl}&facail={word}
```

When Multidict looks up a word, it substitutes the relevant sl and tl. The tl field in the `dictParam` record for the n×n dictionary also contains a "¤" symbol if this is truly an n×n dictionary, including monolingual pairs such as English-English. If it is actually an "n×(n-1)" dictionary excluding monolingual pairs, this is denoted by placing instead an "x" in the tl field.

2.6 Quality ranking

To try to place the "best" dictionaries at the top of the list in the user interface, and also to ensure that the "best" dictionary for the language-pair is used by default, the `dictParam` table stores a "quality" figure for each dictionary. Of course, this is necessarily a compromise. What is best for one purpose might not be best for another. And things get messy when it comes to n×n dictionaries. Multidict already records and defaults to the previous dictionary which the user used for that language-pair. It might be best, instead of over-relying on a "quality" figure, to extend this recording system to the second and third most recent dictionaries used, or perhaps move to a system based on usage statistics.

2.7 Web Archive dictionaries

Online dictionary resources are often very scarce for minority languages. However, many excellent old paper dictionaries are now available in page-image format on the Web Archive at `www.archive.org`[24], and also on Google Books[25]. The wonderful thing is that these dictionaries

[20] http://multidict.net/multidict/languages.php
[21] http://multitree.linguistlist.org
[22] http://glosbe.com
[23] http://www.globalglossary.org
[24] https://archive.org/details/texts

can be addressed by url on an individual page basis. So all we need to do to make the dictionary available via Multidict is to provide Multidict with a table giving it the first word on every page of the dictionary. Or actually, the last word on every page works slightly better because of the technicality that several headwords can have the same spelling. Providing such a table sounds like a daunting task, but in fact, by getting very ergonomically organized the time can be reduced to a few seconds per page, meaning that even a 1000 page dictionary can be dealt with in a few hours. To date, 23 such page-image dictionaries have been made available via Multidict (counting the reverse direction separately in 5 cases), namely 8 for Scottish Gaelic; 2 Irish; 1 Old Irish; 3 Manx; 1 Cornish; 1 Old English; 1 Middle English; 3 Nyanja and 3 Maori. In total, about 55,000 pages have been indexed. The biggest example is that all 4323 columns of the Old Irish eDIL[26] dictionary have been indexed, and in fact eDIL is currently more usable for most purposes via Multidict than using its own native search interface. Although the native search will search the whole dictionary, which can sometimes be wonderfully useful, it will find nothing at all if the search word is not specified exactly as written in the dictionary, including all accents and hyphens. With the vagaries of Old Irish spelling, it can be more useful to take the user to the right spot in alphabetic order as Multidict does, leaving him or her to complete the search by eye.

To enable access to these page-image dictionaries, Multidict uses two tables, `dictPage` which records the first (or last) word on every page, and `dictPageURL` which records the url templates required to translate these page numbers into urls. The mechanism can also cope with dictionaries which are split into several volumes, as is Dwelly in the Web Archive . A program `dictpage.php` does the job of redirecting the browser to the appropriate url.

2.8 Statistics

Multidict currently handles 271 different online dictionaries - there are 271 records in the `dict` table. The dictParam table has 2101 records covering 1041 language pairs, but the numbers would be tens of thousands higher if the n×n dictionaries Glosbe and Global Glossary were included. Multidict currently handles 202 languges, or 140 if the n×n dictionaries are excluded.

3 Wordlink

3.1 The interface

In the example shown below, Wordlink is being used to view the Irish Wikipedia homepage. At the top is the Wordlink navigation frame which is used for control. Below that is a frame with what looks exactly like the Wikipedia page, but it is in fact a doctored version, with the html modifed by Wordlink to link every word to online dictionaries via Multidict, as shown on the right.

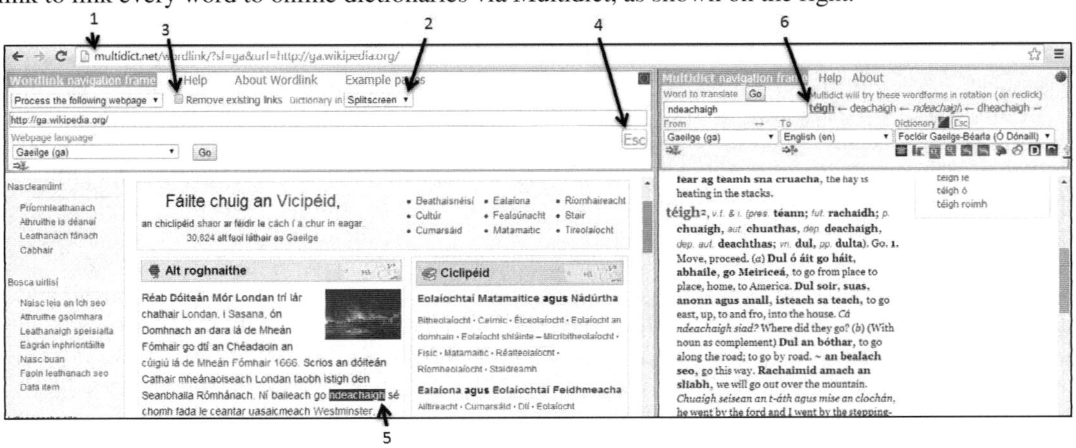

Figure 2. The Wordlink interface

[25] http://books.google.com
[26] http://edil.qub.ac.uk/dictionary/search.php

Note (**1**) the **url**:
`http://multidict.net/wordlink/?sl=ga&url=http://ga.wikipedia.org/`
which can be used to refer to the wordlinked page. An additional paramater `navsize=1` can be used to reduce the navigation frame away to 1 pixel size if it is not required. If the url is specified in the form `url=referer`, the url is taken from the referer information in the http request. This means that by adding a link of this form to every page of a website, each page is linked to a Wordlinked version of itself for the benefit of language learners. This can be seen in use on the Fòram na Gàidhlig[27] website.

Note (**2**) the choice of **mode**, "Splitscreen" which causes Multidict and the dictionary results to be shown in a frame on the right. Wordlink has three other choices of mode available "New tab", "Same tab" and "Popup". Although Splitscreen is the default and is overwhelmingly the most used, the other modes could actually be very useful on smaller screens.

Note (**3**) the option to "**Remove existing links**". By default, Wordlink does not actually link every word to a dictionary lookup. If you click on the word *Dóitean*, it will take you instead to a Wordlinked version of the *Dóiteán Mór Londan* Wikipedia page. "Remove existing links" does what it says and will instead ensure you are taken to a dictionary lookup of *Dóiteán*.

Note (**4**) the **Esc** button. Wordlink like Multidict makes it easy for you to escape from its frames to the webpage itself.

Note (**5**) that the word *ndeachaigh* has been clicked on to find it in the dictionary, and it is therefore **highlighted** and remains highlighted until another word is clicked. This small point is of major importance. Very often the user will need to scroll the dictionary information (as indeed in this example), and it is essential that the word be highlighted to make it easy to look back and continue reading.

Note (**6**) that although Multidict has been handed the wordform *ndeachaigh* by Wordlink, it has chosen instead to look up *téigh*, which it thinks is probably the appropriate "lemma", the dictionary headword to look up, and it has also lined up a row of other lemma suggestions to be tried in turn if the user reclicks "ndeachaigh" or clicks "Go" in Multidict. This new **lemmatization** feature built into Multidict has resulted in a big improvement in the user experience when using Wordlink and Clilstore. Some online dictionaries can do their own lemmatization, but many good dictionaries do not. And even when the dictionary itself offers excellent lemmatization suggestions, as does *Ó Dónaill*[28] in the example above, the new "click to retry" feature is so slick to use that it can be much quicker to just reclick and let Multidict do the work. The feature is described more fully in section 3.4 below.

3.2 The Wordlink program

The Wordlink program, like all the facilities at `multidict.net` is written in PHP[29]. It first sends off an HTTP request to fetch the webpage to be processed. It then converts it to UTF-8 character encoding[30] if it is not already in UTF-8, because all the facilities work internally entirely in UTF-8. It then processes the page to (1) convert existing links into links to Wordlinked pages (if this has not been switched off by "Remove existing links"), and (2) convert each word in runs of text into a link to make Multidict look up that word. We will not go into the details, but suffice it to say that it is not an easy task, and it is essential to ensure that relative links to images, stylesheets and Javascript libraries are all appropriately converted. It currently works by processing the html serially, but it would probably be better to convert it to use an html parser and then traverse the resulting DOM tree.

Wordlink does not work well with all webpages, particularly flashy games pages or TV company websites and suchlike. But it produces good to excellent results with a good 90% of the more textual webpages likely to be of interest to language learners. With well-behaved pages such as Wikipedia it works perfectly. It does not work at all with webpages requiring a login, such as Facebook or pages in virtual-learning environments. To do this would require it to store and forward user-credentials and would get us into the very iffy field of trust relationships. Nor does it work with the https (secure http) protocol.

---

27 http://www.foramnagaidhlig.net/foram/
28 http://breis.focloir.ie/ga/fgb/
29 http://www.php.net
30 http://en.wikipedia.org/wiki/UTF-8

3.3 Word segmentation

Wordlink links "words" to dictionaries, and for most languages it identifies words by the whitespace or punctuation characters surrounding them. This means that it does not deal with collocations or phrases or even hyphenated words such as "trade-union". In such cases, the user can always type additional text into the Multidict search box. But it would be nice if some sort of Javascript or browser extension could be devised to allow the user to select phrases with the mouse and look them up.

Breton and **Catalan** presented Wordlink with a slight problem, because "c'h" in Breton is regarded as a letter, as is "l·l" in Catalan, and at first Wordlink was splitting the word at what it thought was a punctuation character. This was easily cured by a small change to the program.

Japanese, Chinese, Korean and Thai webpages present it with the much bigger problem that these languages are normally written without any space between "words". However, we have newly built into it an interface with the **Japanese** word segmenter **Mecab**[31]. This seems to be successful, and gives the spinoff benefit that hovering over a Japanese word now displays its pronunciation in Hiragana. Japanese learners have such a hard task to face with unknown Kanji that even partial success could be of tremendous benefit. For **Chinese**, we managed to do the same with the **Urheen**[32] word segmenter and the results seem to be good, but at the time of writing this is performing far too slowly to be useful and has been switched off. The bother seems to be that Urheen does a lot of inefficient initialization every time it is called, but we might manage to find ways round this.

3.4 The "lemmatization" facility in Multidict

Although this belongs to Multidict as regards programming, it is described here because it is when Multidict is used together with Wordlink that all sorts of inflected wordforms are thrown at it. We put "lemmatization" in inverted commas, because the facility is only semi-trying to produce grammatical lemmas. Because it is only going to present the user with a string of possibilities, it does not need to go for grammatical purity and "headword suggestions" might be a better term than lemmas.

The basis of this facility in Multidict for most source languages is the **Hunspell**[33] spellchecker, which is the opensource spellchecker used by LibreOffice, OpenOffice, Firefox, etc. Old-fashioned spellcheckers just had a long list of wordforms in a .dic file. Hunspell, on the other hand, was originally developed for Hungarian which is a highly inflected language and works in a much more intelligent way using also a .aff file (aff<affix). The words in the .dic file can be labelled for grammatical category, and the .aff file contains the rules to produce a range of inflected wordforms relevant to that grammatical category. The great thing is that we do not need to attempt to understand or reverse engineer these rules. Hunspell itself has built into it a function to return the possible lemmas corresponding to any given wordform. All we need to do is to pull in from the Internet the Hunspell .dic and .aff files for lots of languages, and this we have done.

How successful Hunspell is at lemmatizing depends on the language and how Hunspell has been implemented for it. It is possible for an implementer to just throw lots of wordforms into the .dic file and put very few rules in the .aff file. Hunspell lemmatizes Basque very well, for example, but the current implementation does very little for German. For Scottish Gaelic it was not great and for Irish not much better, and so we turned to another solution, the use of a **lemmatization table**.

We were very fortunate and very grateful to be donated huge lemmatization tables for both Scottish Gaelic and Irish. And a huge public domain table for Italian, Morph-it[34] (Zanchetta and Baroni, 2005), was found on the Internet. Smaller batches added to this include the Old Irish verbforms from In Dúil Bélrai[35]; tables from the Internet converting between en-US and en-GB English spelling; and tables converting between pre-Caighdeán and post-Caighdeán Irish spelling. These form the basis of an alternative method of lemmatization which Multidict has at its disposal, namely the `lemmas` table in the Multidict database which currently has 1.4 million wordforms. These can be labelled with the "batch"

---

[31] http://mecab.googlecode.com

[32] http://www.openpr.org.cn/index.php/NLP-Toolkit-For-Natural-Language-Processing/68-Urheen-A-Chinese/English-Lexical-Analysis-Toolkit/View-details.html

[33] http://hunspell.sourceforge.net

[34] http://sslmitdev-online.sslmit.unibo.it/linguistics/morph-it.php

[35] http://www.smo.uhi.ac.uk/sengoidelc/duil-belrai/

field, which can be used for example to denote those to be given priority, or those to be applied only for certain dictionaries.

Algorithmic "lemmatization" provides yet another tool in Multidict's lemmatization armoury. Again this is divided into a "priority" algorithm to be used first, and a non-priority algorithm. The priority algorithm includes the removal of initial mutations from Irish and Scottish Gaelic words, because this is nearly always something sensible to do. The non-priority algorithm includes throwing out any final 's' from English words, because this is normally a last resort when the word has not been recognized by Hunspell. The non-priority algorithm includes crude attempts to lemmatize words in the p-celtic languages, Welsh, Cornish and Breton, by naively changing the initial letter.

It turns out to be rather crucial, especially for Irish and Scottish Gaelic, to have priority records in the the `lemmas` table for the lemmatization of **irregular** verbs, otherwise many of them would not be recognised after initial mutation was removed. This has been done, and all the prepositional pronouns have been added too. This is something we really ought to do for every language: namely feed into the lemmatization table all the irregular verbs, irregular nouns, etc, because Hunspell deals with these rather poorly. Hunspell's priorities and ours are different. Its priority is to reduce the size of the .dic file by placing rules for regular verbs and nouns in the .aff file. Irregular verbforms take up relatively little space in the .dic file, so it just throws them in there and doesn't help us at all to lemmatize them. Multidict now has in place a very sophisticated, flexible mechanism for lemmatization, pulling in as required the different tools at its disposal. It would be good if experts for individual languages could co-operate to help implement and tailor these tools for each particular language.

The default "wfrule" string which Multidict uses to generate headword suggestions for a particular wordform is "`lemtable~pri|prialg|self|lemtable|hun|lemalg`". What this means in plain English is: concatenate the lists of headword suggestions produced by (1) those labelled "pri" in the `lemmas` table, (2) those produced by the priority algorithm, (3) the wordform itself, (4) those with no batch label in `lemmas`, (5) those provided by Hunspell, and (6) those produced by the non-priority algorithm. The | operator not only concatenates but causes duplicates to be removed from the list. However, different "wfrule" strings can be applied for different languages and dictionaries. As well as the | operator, there is another operator > which causes the array of suggestions generated by the previous rule to be used as input to a following rule. And brackets ( ) can also be used in this "algebra".

3.5 Beware of robots

In any publicly available facility such as Wordlink which can take any webpage and process it to produce another, it is essential to be very careful about `robots.txt`[36] and robots meta tags in the html header. At one point the server hosting multidict.net was running very slowly and on investigation it was found that Google was attempting to spider and index the entire Internet via Wordlink! The links on one Wordlinked webpage were leading it to other Wordlinked webpages. It took months before it completely stopped.

4 Clilstore

Clilstore is the most recent of the three facilities. It makes it easy for teachers to harness the power of Wordlink and Multidict, by adding teaching "units" to the openly available online "store". The formula which has been found to be most successful has been a video or soundfile together with a transcript, and perhaps some exercises to test student understanding. Clilstore itself stores the text, and can store attachment files of limited size. But storing the video or soundfile is left to the very many media hosting services available on the Internet, such as Youtube, Vimeo, TED, Teachertube, Ipadio and Soundcloud, from where they can be very easily added to the Clilstore unit by using the embed code supplied by the hosting service. This avoids us getting into large storage requirements, and hives off any copyright questions to services with mechanisms in place to deal with infringements.

Each unit is labelled with a level, A1, A2, B1, B2, C1 or C2, from the Common European Framework of Reference for languages (CEFR[37]). The index provides a rich facility for searching by words

36 http://en.wikipedia.org/wiki/Robots_exclusion_standard

37 http://en.wikipedia.org/wiki/Common_European_Framework_of_Reference_for_Languages
http://www.coe.int/t/dg4/linguistic/Cadre1_en.asp

in the title or text, and for searching or ordering by language, CEFR, media length, number of words, number of views, etc. A wysiwyg editor, **TinyMCE**[38], provides a facility for authors to produce rich colourful units without getting involved in html, although an html editor is also available.

To date (2014-06-24), Clilstore has 1072 units (excluding test units) in 49 different languages. The biggest number (416) are in English, but there are 116 in Arabic, 101 in Scottish Gaelic, 65 in Slovenian, 51 in Irish, 40 in Portuguese, 38 in Spanish, 34 in Italian, 27 in Lithuanian, 26 in German, 22 in Danish. There is even one, complete with soundfile in Old Irish. Clilstore and Wordlink work fine with right-to-left languages such as Arabic, although good online dictionaries are still rather lacking for Arabic. Statistics show that the units have had so far over 203,000 views in total. Perhaps more interestingly and reliably, in the 3 months since we started collecting such statistics, there have been 6773 clicks (dictionary lookups) on words in Clilstore units.

Experience from workshops for Gaelic language summer courses[39] at various levels at Sabhal Mòr Ostaig shows that the Clilstore facility is most useful to intermediate level learners. Advanced users find it very useful too, as a store of videos and transcripts, but tend to click fairly seldom because they can understand well enough from context anyway. Learners coming from **cognate languages** with somewhat different spelling rules such as Irish learners of Scottish Gaelic find it particularly useful, as was seen on the summer courses on Scottish Gaelic for Irish speakers at Sabhal Mòr Ostaig.

5 Conclusion

The facilities described here work, have proved their worth[40], and are freely and openly available. Much more could be done to develop them, of course. The interface is entirely through English at present, which is not good when trying to provide an immersion environment for Gaelic students, for example. Nor is good for Italian students at a Portuguese university, to have to go through an English interface to access Portuguese units. It would be good to internationalize the programs and provide localized interfaces.

Multidict and Wordlink use old-fashioned html frames[41], which have no support in modern standards[42], although they work well for the job in hand. It would be good to investigate switching to iframes[43], although this would require increasing use of Javascript libraries for resizing.

Users can and do recommend new dictionaries for Multidict, but it would be good to develop this into more of a community facility.

Acknowledgements

Multidict and Wordlink were first developed under the EC financed[44] POOLS-T[45] project. Clilstore was developed, and Multidict and Wordlink further developed under TOOLS[46] project financed by the EC's Lifelong Learning Programme. Much of the credit for their development goes to the suggestions, user testing and feedback by the project teams from 9 different European countries, and in particular to the project leader Kent Andersen. Wordlink was inspired by Kent's Textblender program. We are grateful to Kevin Scannell for the Irish lemmatization table used by Multidict, and to Mìcheal Bauer and Will Robertson for the Scottish Gaelic lemmatization table.

References

Eros Zanchetta and Marco Baroni.. 2005. *Morph-it! A free corpus-based morphological resource for the Italian language*, proceedings of Corpus Linguistics 2005, University of Birmingham, Birmingham, UK

---

38 http://www.tinymce.com

39 http://www.smo.uhi.ac.uk/gd/cursaichean/cursaichean-goirid

40 There are now 1072 Clilstore units, and new are created almost daily both by people inside the project and people completely unconnected with it. Wordlink has clocked up over 315,000 dictionary lookups in the past six years.

41 http://www.w3.org/TR/html401/present/frames.html

42 http://www.w3.org/TR/html5/obsolete.html

43 http://www.w3.org/TR/html5/embedded-content-0.html#the-iframe-element

44 Standard disclaimer applies: This publication reflects the views only of the author, and the Commission cannot be held responsible for any use which may be made of the information contained therein

45 http://languages.dk/pools-t

46 http://languages.dk/tools

Processing Mutations in Breton with Finite-State Transducers

Thierry Poibeau
Laboratoire LATTICE (UMR8094)
CNRS & Ecole normale supérieure & Université Paris 3 Sorbonne Nouvelle
1 rue Maurice Arnoux 92120 Montrouge France
thierry.poibeau@ens.fr

Abstract

One characteristic feature of Celtic languages is mutation, i.e. the fact that the initial consonant of words may change according to the context. We provide a quick description of this linguistic phenomenon for Breton along with a formalization using finite state transducers. This approach allows an exact and compact description of mutations. The result can be used in various contexts, especially for spell checking and language teaching.

1 Introduction

Celtic languages (Welsh, Cornish, Irish, Scottish-Gaelic, Manx, etc.) are known to support a common feature: the initial consonant of different types of words (esp. nouns, adjectives and verbs) is modified in certain contexts and after certain function words (e.g. prepositions and determiners for nouns and adjectives; auxiliaries for verbs). This phenomenon known as "mutation" has been largely studied and described from a linguistic point of view. Formal descriptions have even been proposed, especially Mittendorf and Sadler (2006) for Welsh.

In this paper, we investigate mutations in Breton.[1] Our study is largely inspired by the previous study by Mittendorf and Sadler for Welsh: We share with these authors the idea that "initial mutation is close to inflection in nature and is essentially a morphosyntactic phenomenon". We propose to process this phenomenon with finite state transducers. In fact, we propose two formalizations: in the first one, mutations are processed by directly storing the lexical forms with mutations in a dictionary of inflected forms; in the second one, local rules encoded using finite state transducers are applied dynamically, depending on the context. We show that this strategy allows for an exact and compact description of the phenomenon, since transducers directly encode grammar rules.

The paper is organized as follows: we first propose a linguistic description of this phenomenon. We then explore the two strategies exposed in the previous paragraph: a dictionary of inflected form vs local grammars encoded using finite state machines. We conclude with a discussion and an overview of the practical use of this implementation.

1.1 A Quick Description of Mutations in Breton

As said in Wikipedia (http://en.wikipedia.org/wiki/Breton_mutations), "Breton is characterized by initial consonant mutations, which are changes to the initial sound of a word caused by certain syntactic or morphological environments. In addition Breton, like French, has a number of purely phonological sandhi features caused when certain sounds come into contact with others." The following details are then added: "the mutations are divided into four main groups, according to the changes they cause: soft mutation (in Breton: *kemmadurioù dre vlotaat*), hard mutation (*kemmadurioù dre galetaat*), spirant mutation (*kemmadurioù c'hwezhadenniñ*) and mixed mutation (*kemmadurioù mesket*). There are also a number of defective (or incomplete) mutations which affect only certain words or certain letters." A

[1] Breton is a Celtic language spoken in Brittany (Western France) According to recent studies, 200,000 persons understand the language but only 35,000 practice it on a daily basis.

Proceedings of the First Celtic Language Technology Workshop, pages 28–32,
Dublin, Ireland, August 23 2014.

same word can thus appear differently depending on these classes of changes (for example the noun *tad – father* – becomes *da dad – your father; he zad – her father*; etc. because of the possessive pronouns *da* and *he* that entail different kinds of mutation).

The best approach to give an idea of mutations is to consider some examples. "Soft mutations" refer to the fact that after the definite article *ar* (and its variant *an*) or the indefinite article *ur* (or *un*) the initial consonant of singular feminine nouns is subject to the following changes:

- K → G, ex. Kador (*chair*) → Ur gador
- T → D, ex. Taol (*table*) → Un daol
- P → B, ex. Paner (*basket*) → Ur baner
- G → C'H, ex. Gavr (*goat*) → Ur c'havr
- GW → W, ex. Gwern (*mast*) → Ur wern

Note that in Breton nouns referring to objects and abstract notions can be either masculine or feminine (there is no neuter case).

Although the phenomenon is well known, its description is not straightforward since it involves a large number of parameters and different types of information (lexical, morphological, semantic). For example, plural masculine nouns referring to male persons have the same behavior as singular feminine nouns (but this is only true for plural masculine nouns referring to people, not for all plural nouns). It is therefore necessary to distinguish different categories of nouns.

- K → G, ex. Kigerien (*butchers*) → Ar gigerien
- T → D, ex. Tud (*people*) → An dud
- P → B, ex. Pesketaerien (*fishermen*) → Ar besketaerien
- G → C'H, ex. Gellaoued (*French*) → Ar C'hallaoued
- GW → W, ex. Gwerzherien (*sellers*) → Ar werzherien

These mutations also affect adjectives, provided that the noun preceding the adjective ends with a vowel or with the consonant l, m, n, or r.

- K → G, ex. Kaer (*nice*) → Ur gador gaer (a nice chair)
- T → D, ex. Tev (*thick*) → Ur wern dev (a thick mast)
- P → B, ex. Paour (*poor*) → Ur vamm baour (a poor mother)

There are different series of mutations depending on the functional word preceding the noun (and the adjectives if any). It is one of the main difficulties of the language since this phenomenon changes the initial of the words: after mutation, words cannot be found anymore directly in the dictionary.

A comprehensive description of this phenomenon can be found in traditional grammars of the language: see especially Kervella (1976), Hemon (1984) and Stump (1984) for a formal description of agreement in Breton.

1.2 Automatic Processing of Mutations in Breton

Two approaches are possible:

- store all the inflected lexical forms and their mutations in a dictionary. Mutation is then considered as a case of word variation (like the alternation singular/plural);
- compute on the fly the lexical form in context, which is an interesting strategy for text generation or, more directly, in the context of text authoring (for example to assist students producing texts in Breton).

In this paper, we consider both approaches since they are both relevant depending on the context.

2 Two Competing / Complementary Solutions for Mutations in Breton

The following section describes two ways of processing mutations in Breton. We discuss their interest and their applicability to the problem.

2.1 A Comprehensive Dictionary of Inflected Forms

This solution is the simplest one: all inflected forms including those with modified initial letters are included in the dictionary. The dictionary remains manageable and ambiguity introduced by the new lexical forms is limited. Below is a short extract of a dictionary of inflected forms including lexical forms after mutation:

```
kador,kador.N:fs          taol,taol.N:fs
gador,kador.N:fs          daol,taol.N:fs
c'hador,kador.N:fs        zaol,taol.N:fs
```

The format of the dictionary is the one defined by LADL (Courtois and Silberztein, 1990): inflected forms are followed by a lemma (separated by a comma). The category of the word can then be found (N for noun) as well as morphosyntactic features (fs: feminine singular).

However, this solution is not fully satisfactory since it does not explain why a given form is used in a given context. It would be relevant to provide a more dynamic description of the process taking into account the different constraints we have seen in the previous section.

2.2 A Finite State Approach

We have seen in the introduction that mutations refer to a simple change in the first letter of certain words in certain contexts. This phenomenon is essentially local (it does not require to take into account a large context) so finite state transducers seem to be a relevant choice. These transducers will directly encode the rules described in the grammar of Breton that just need to be made more formal.

Below (Figure 1) is an example of such a finite state transducer.

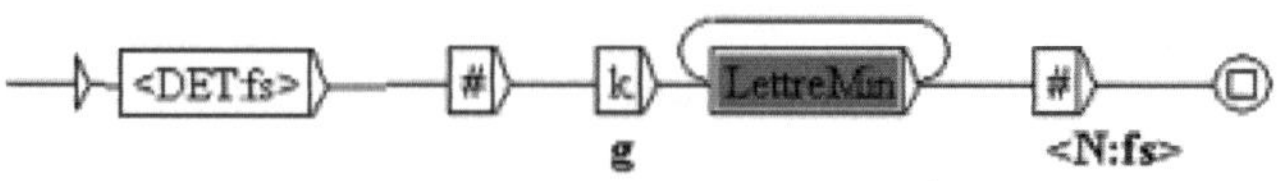

Figure 1: Graph MUT-Detfs-K-G

This graph directly encodes all the constraints involved in the process. Elements that appear in boxes describe a linguistic sequence while elements appearing under the boxes correspond to the rewriting part of the transducer (i.e. the transduction). Here is a description of the different elements that can be used for the linguistic description:

- Tags between < and > refer to morphosyntactic categories (DET for determiner, N for noun, A for adjective, etc.);
- The elements after the colon are morphological features (f: feminine , s: singular...);
- The # sign indicates a separator between words (e.g. blank spaces between words);
- A gray box refers to a subgraph (here LettreMin refers to all lowercase letters; please note that the sequence described here corresponds to any sequence of letters between separators, i.e. tokens, because of the recursion on the state itself);
- Other items appearing in a box correspond to characters (or lexical forms);

Here, we see clearly that K becomes G if the sequence is a fem. sing. noun appearing immediately after a determiner. Notations correspond to the ones defined by the LADL team, see Silberztein (1993) and Paumier (2011) – other frameworks could of course be used like the Xerox FST toolbox (Beesley and Karttunen, 2003).

Transducers provide a unified view of the different contraints along with a rewriting process. Recursive transducers (RTN) make it possible to obtain a concise and effective formalization. Different linguistic phenomena can be processed using a cascade of automata applied one after the other. For example, it seems relevant to re-use the graph encoding noun mutations to process adjectives. If all the mutations for nouns have been encoded and compiled in a single graph called MUT, it is then possible to write the fllowing transducer (figure 2) for adjectives.

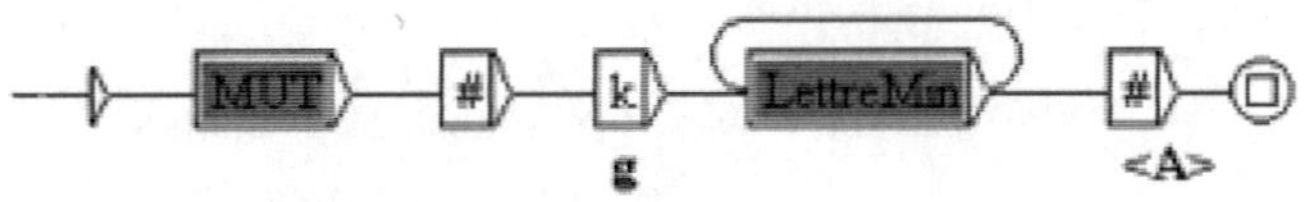

Figure 2: Graph MUT-Adj-K-G

MUT also encodes the constraints on the last vowel of the previous word (only adjectives following a noun ending with a vowel or with l, m, n or r are subject to this mutation).

2.3 Implementation and evaluation

Local contextual grammars can be encoded using various techniques but finite state transducers seem to be the most effective and readable way to encode these rules. This is in line with previous work: for example Mittendorf and Sadler (2006) use the Xerox finite state transducer toolbox to implement mutations in Welsh. Our proposal is very close to theirs.

Various other platforms allow the manipulation of finite state transducers for local grammars. Scripting languages (like perl or python) also offer a good solution but these languages are made to manipulate strings. However for mutations we need to have different information on the words themselves, hence using a linguistic toolbox seems more appropriate.

The implementation of this linguistic phenomenon using finite state transducers produce a compact and accurate description. Grammars are easy to modify and maintain. Additionally different grammars could be developed to take into account local variations and dialects.

3 Discussion

We have presented a practical approach to process mutations in breton. The approach is based on well known techniques (finite state transducers) that provide an accurate and efficient description of the phenomenon. The technique used reveal the fact that mutation is essentially a morphosyntactic phenomenon, as said in the introduction.

However, the main challenge does not lie in the proposed formalization. Endangered languages are generally not well supported (lack of resources and automatic tools) and we think this kind of contribution could have a positive impact on the evolution of the language. If relevant tools exist, it could be a way to attract new attention and help language students acquire a good command of the language. Since a large part of language learners study at home, having dynamic tools assisting text production would be a real plus.

Adding explanation to the above rules would make it possible to generate suggestions during text production or text revision. From this perspective, the description we provide could serve as a basis for a spell checker of the language.[2] Detailed explanations would make the whole system usable for assisting people during language learning (e.g. to explain why a given sequence in not fully correct in case a word should appear with a mutation, etc.). This strategy could easily be re-used for other languages and other linguistic phenomena.

[2]Note that different initiatives exist to develop natural language tools for processing Breton. We should cite more specifically the association Drouizig http://www.drouizig.org/ that has developed a spell checker independently of this study.

References

Kenneth R. Beesley and Lauri Karttunen. 2003. *Finite State Morphology*. CSLI Publications, Stanford.

Blandine Courtois and Max Silberztein, editors. 1990. *Dictionnaires lectroniques du français*, volume 87, Paris. Larousse.

Roparz Hemon. 1984. *Grammaire bretonne*. Al Liamm, Brest.

Fransez Kervella. 1976. *Yezhadur bras ar brezhoneg*. Al Liamm, Brest.

Ingo Mittendorf and Louisa Sadler. 2006. A treatment of welsh initial mutations. In *Proceedings of the LFG06 Conference*, Universität Konstanz. CSLI.

Sébastien Paumier. 2011. *Unitex 3.0 User Manual*. Universit de Marne la Vallée, Marne la Vallée.

Max Silberztein. 1993. *Dictionnaires lectroniques et analyse automatique de textes : le systme INTEX*. Masson, Paris.

Gregory Stump. 1984. Agreement vs. incorporation in breton. *Natural Language and Linguistic Theory*, 2:289–348.

Statistical models for text normalization and machine translation

Kevin Scannell
Department of Mathematics and Computer Science
Saint Louis University
St. Louis, Missouri, USA
kscanne@gmail.com

Abstract

Irish and Scottish Gaelic are closely-related languages that together with Manx Gaelic make up the Goidelic branch of the Celtic family. We present a statistical model for translation from Scottish Gaelic to Irish that we hope will facilitate communication between the two language communities, especially in social media. An important aspect of this work is to overcome the orthographical differences between the languages, many of which were introduced in a major spelling reform of Irish in the 1940's and 1950's. Prior to that date, the orthographies of the two languages were quite similar, thanks in part to a shared literary tradition. As a consequence of this, machine translation from Scottish Gaelic to Irish has a great deal in common with the problem of normalizing pre-standard Irish texts, a problem with applications to lexicography and information retrieval. We show how a single statistical model can be used effectively in both contexts.

1 Introduction

Irish and Scottish Gaelic are closely-related languages in the Celtic language family. Each is spoken as the day-to-day language by minority communities in Ireland and Scotland, respectively. While each language can be considered "under-resourced" in terms of language technology when compared with English, French, Spanish, etc., they are significantly better-off than many European minority languages, and far ahead of most indigenous languages of Australia, Africa, and the Americas (Judge et al., 2012), (Bauer, 2014).

Our primary aim in this paper is to describe a machine translation (MT) engine for translating from Scottish Gaelic into Irish. This is not the first time this language pair has been considered in the literature. We developed a rule-based system for translating between these two languages almost ten years ago, but in the opposite direction (Scannell, 2006). Some of that work has since been ported to the Apertium MT framework (Corbí-Bellot et al., 2005), (Forcada et al., 2011), and in particular is now available as free software; because of this we were able to reuse those resources in the present project. We believe strongly in open source approaches to language technology development for minority languages, and so the source code and lexicons for the present project are all freely available under the GPL.[1]

Our secondary aim is to apply the same statistical model to an equally important language-processing challenge, namely the standardization of historical Irish texts. The Irish language underwent a major spelling reform in the 1940's and 1950's with the introduction of the the so-called *Caighdeán Oifigiúil* (Official Standard) by the Irish government. The Official Standard succeeded in simplifying the orthography in a number of ways, and has been almost universally adopted in textbooks, government publications, and by the news media. On the other hand, from the perspective of a language technologist, it has caused great difficulties. For example, pre-standard texts are rendered invisible to search engines when users search via standard spellings. And a tremendous amount of high-quality writing by native Irish speakers

[1]See https://github.com/kscanne/caighdean.

Proceedings of the First Celtic Language Technology Workshop, pages 33–40,
Dublin, Ireland, August 23 2014.

(tens of millions of words) produced between about 1925 and 1945 is effectively unusable for language modeling or other NLP applications.

This explains the importance of Irish standardization, but what does it have to do with Scottish Gaelic–Irish MT? The answer is twofold: first, we can cast the standardization problem as an MT problem between two *very* closely-related languages (namely, pre-standard and standard Irish), and second, the orthography of pre-standard Irish has a great deal in common with the orthography of Scottish Gaelic, and so it turns out that a single statistical model works well to solve both problems. A brief description of the standardizer has appeared previously in (Uí Dhonnchadha et al., 2014), as part of a more complex pipeline for processing historical Irish texts for lexicography.

Many authors have considered MT between closely-related language pairs, including dozens of papers describing rule-based systems based on the Apertium engine (Forcada et al., 2011).[2] Several other papers have taken statistical or hybrid approaches, e.g. (Hajič, 2000) for Czech and Slovak, (Altintas and Cicekli, 2002) for Turkish and Crimean Tatar, (Nakov and Tiedemann, 2012) for Macedonian and Bulgarian, and (Miller, 2008) and the references therein. Statistical MT techniques have also been used previously for historical text normalization; see for example (Pettersson et al., 2013).

The outline of the paper is as follows: In section 2, we describe the shared statistical model in general terms, and discuss the problematic notion of "standard Irish". In section 3 we describe `gd2ga`, our Scottish Gaelic–Irish MT system, along with the parallel corpus used in its development. Finally, in section 4, we introduce and evaluate the Irish standardizer.

2 The Model

In this section we describe the statistical model that underlies both the `gd2ga` machine translation system and the Irish standardizer. We view both problems as instances of machine translation between very closely-related languages, the latter requiring translation from what we will call "pre-standard Irish" to "standard Irish" (with scare quotes because both terms are problematic; more on this below). Because of the limited syntactic differences between source and target in each case, it suffices to use a simple word-based model without reordering, a variant of the well-known IBM model 1 (Brown et al., 1993). It is important to distinguish the statistical model per se (which assigns probabilities to translation candidates) from the means by which those probabilities are acquired. In the context of the IBM models, Expectation Maximization (EM) is typically used for the latter; here we take a simpler approach, described in section 2.2. In the two subsections that follow, we will describe the language model and translation model, respectively.

2.1 Language Model

The target language in both cases is what we are calling "standard Irish", and so a single language model suffices for both systems. We use a trigram model which is typical in this context and normally would require little further comment. In our situation, however, we run into a couple of major difficulties.

First, there is not complete agreement with respect to what "standard Irish" means. The first movement toward standardization of the written language goes back to the 1930's with the establishment of government committees to look at the question. A simplified spelling system was published in 1945 (Rannóg an Aistriúcháin, 1945) and implemented by the government translation office around the same time. A simplified grammar was published in 1958 (Rannóg an Aistriúcháin, 1958), followed by two important bilingual dictionaries (de Bhaldraithe, 1959; Ó Dónaill, 1977) that helped encourage use of the standard language by the general public. The problem is that these dictionaries do not completely conform to the published standard, nor do many grammar books that are used in schools and by independent learners even today. To compond the confusion, a revised version of the official standard was recently published (Uíbh Eachach, 2012), and has been criticized by some in the language community (Mac Lochlainn, 2012), so it remains to be seen the extent to which it will be embraced as the new "standard Irish".

The second difficulty is that, even to the extent that everyone agrees on certain elements of the standard, *no one* implements them completely in their writing, which is to say that virtually all non-trivial texts in

[2]For the most up-to-date references, see `http://wiki.apertium.org/wiki/Publications`.

Irish contain some non-standard forms. In the case of `gd2ga`, this is not of great concern; we could train the target language model with the texts we have, and the output would resemble the fluent, natural Irish of the training texts. For the standardizer, however, we are aiming at very high precision, with the output conforming to *some* version of the standard. In short, the problem is this: we want to train an n-gram model for a certain language, but there are *no non-trivial texts written in that language*.

We get around these issues by making use of a suite of open-source Irish language proofing tools called *An Gramadóir*.[3] From an initial corpus of about 100 million words, we selected a subset of about 40 million words comprised of the texts that are most conformant to the standard. To do this, the rules implemented in *An Gramadóir* were first separated into those representing true "errors" (misspellings, grammatical mistakes, etc.) from those representing standardizations. Then, *An Gramadóir* was run on every text in the corpus in order to assign each a numerical measure of "non-standardness" (the number of standardizations flagged per 100 words). The subcorpus was chosen from the texts with the lowest non-standardness scores. Finally, we applied a small number of automated substitutions to certain non-standard forms that are nearly as common as their standardizations in real-world texts, e.g. *nach dtáinig* vs. *nár tháinig* ("did not come").

Once the training corpus is generated in this way, we tokenize and compute the probabilities for the trigram language model (no pruning), and smooth using absolute discounting (Chen and Goodman, 1996). The implementation of the language model is included as part of the translator itself in order to avoid external dependencies on libraries such as IRSTLM, KenLM, etc.

2.2 Translation Model

The translation model represents the conditional probability of some source language word corresponding to a given target language word. Since the parallel corpora for our two translation problems are relatively small, and since our goal is very high-precision translation, a statistical word alignment approach using Expectation Maximization does not give suitable results. Instead, we take advantage of the resources that we have at hand; specifically, high-quality bilingual lexicons together with a well-understood set of spelling rules for mapping source language words to cognates in the target language. In the context of Scottish Gaelic to Irish MT, the latter include mappings like *-chd* $\longrightarrow$ *-cht* and *-eu-* $\longrightarrow$ *-éa-* (together these two rules map a word like *creuchd* ("wound") to its Irish cognate *créacht* for example). For Irish standardization, there is a separate set of rules but with significant overlap, e.g. *-idhea-* $\longrightarrow$ *-ío-*, which maps *buidheach* ("thankful") to *buíoch* and *fuidheall* ("remainder") to *fuíoll*. These last two examples are valid for both `gd2ga` and for the standardizer.

A source-to-target language mapping is often discovered through a combination of rule-based spelling changes like the ones above, plus a lexical mapping when the rules do not suffice. We define the translation model in the following simple way: (1) all source language words that are paired with a given target language word are assumed to have the same conditional probability; and (2) when a source language word is paired with a target language word by applying some number n of spelling rules, we multiply the conditional probability by a fixed "penalty" β^n. When more than one sequence of rules leads to the same target word, we take the shortest sequence. The constant β was optimized through a tuning process using held-out data from the parallel corpora; we used the value of β which gave the smallest word-error rate on the held-out test set.

Choices (1) and (2) above were made for the sake of simplicity. In future work, we plan to experiment with allowing different probabilities for different rules, as well as using EM to train the translation probabilities, restricting to the lexicographical translation pairs.

The decoding process is quite simple. The algorithm processes the source sentence word-for-word from left-to-right, and keeps track of all possible target language hypotheses along with their probabilities, as computed using the translation model and language model. When multiple hypotheses share the same final two words, we are able to discard all but the one with the highest probability. When we reach the end of the sentence, the highest probability candidate is output as the translation.

[3] See `http://borel.slu.edu/gramadoir/`

3 Scottish Gaelic to Irish MT

Scottish Gaelic and Irish are are sufficiently distinct as spoken languages that even fluent speakers without experience in the other language are usually only able to understand bits and pieces. As a result, there are very few spoken-language contexts in which Scottish Gaelic and Irish speakers are able to interact with each other in either language, and often have to resort to English.[4]

The written language is significantly easier, even in light of the Irish spelling reform and more recent reforms on the Scottish Gaelic side (Scottish Qualifications Authority, 2009) which have made things more difficult than they might conceivably be. Indeed, there are vibrant online communities of Irish and Scottish Gaelic speakers availing themselves of social media, especially Facebook and Twitter, and there is evidence of a significant amount of bilingual communication going on between the two language communities. (Scannell, 2013)

We believe there could be even more, given the right tools. By implementing high-quality Scottish Gaelic to Irish machine translation, and by deploying it in combination with our earlier *ga2gd* system, we hope to encourage greater communication between the two communities.

3.1 Parallel Corpus

A parallel corpus plays a key role in the development of the bilingual lexicon and spelling rules, as well as being used for evaluation purposes. Unfortunately, direct translations between the two languages are extremely rare (despite the relative ease with which such translations could be made), and even translations of a common English source text proved hard to come by. So we chose to include quite a bit of material that might otherwise have been left out of a parallel corpus: software translations (Firefox, LibreOffice, etc.), poetry, song lyrics, prayers, bilingual word lists, Irish glosses on Scottish Gaelic source material (and vice versa), bilingual tweets, titles of linked Wikipedia pages, and so on. When combined with more traditional material (Bible texts, fiction and non-fiction prose translations), we were able to assemble roughly a million words of parallel text: 129,983 translation segments containing 1,016,041 words of Scottish Gaelic and 956,598 words of Irish. This is, to our knowledge, the only non-trivial parallel corpus for this language pair.[5]

3.2 Bilingual Lexicography

The heart of the system is the bilingual lexicon which is being painstakingly constructed by hand (work in progress), drawing upon a number of freely available resources for both languages. Even though the translation system does no part-of-speech tagging, the lexicon stores lemmas in Scottish Gaelic tagged by part-of-speech, mapped to lemmas in Irish, also tagged by part-of-speech. Then, mappings between surface forms are produced by employing morphological generators on both sides (cf. (Tyers, 2009)). This produces mappings for over 150,000 surface forms from a bilingual lexicon with about 13,000 lemmas.

We have used the following resources while building the lexicon.

- The parallel corpus described in section 3.1
- Scottish Gaelic–English dictionaries created by Michael Bauer (Bauer, 2014)
- Various Scottish Gaelic–English dictionaries hosted by Sabhal Mòr Ostaig[6]
- The bilingual lexicon created for (Scannell, 2006)

[4]This despite the efforts of organizations like *Colmcille* (formerly *Iomairt Cholm Cille*), established to encourage precisely this sort of interaction.

[5]We have made the portions of the corpus that are under open licenses available here `http://borel.slu.edu/pub/ccgg.zip`.

[6]See `http://www2.smo.uhi.ac.uk/gaidhlig/faclair/`.

3.3 Evaluation

We began by evaluating the coverage of the source language lexicon. For this, we gathered a monolingual Scottish Gaelic corpus comprised of 3.9M tokens from 14713 web-crawled texts (Scannell, 2007). The system recognized 96.74% of the tokens in this corpus, a result which is comparable to, or even better than, the coverage of many open-source spell checkers on (noisy) web texts. This result is due to (1) the fact that we were able to re-purpose a number of open-source lexical resources when building our dictionary, (2) the addition of a large database of "untranslatables": proper names (e.g. *Facebook*, *Akerbeltz*), non-Gaelic words (mostly English, but some Latin, French, etc.), and abbreviations (e.g. *km*, *vs*) and (3) the ability of the system to handle misspellings and variants either by including them in the lexicon (with mappings to "standard" forms) or through the application of spelling rules.

Evaluating the MT system itself proved problematic. Even though we were able to assemble a parallel corpus, the vast majority of the texts are translations from a common English source (principally, the open-source software translations and the Bible texts), as opposed to direct translations between Irish and Scottish Gaelic. To get around this issue, the author manually translated a collection of 593 sentences from Scottish Gaelic to Irish and used this as a test corpus. When comparing the output of `gd2ga` with these reference translations, the word-error rate (WER) was 38.67%. This can be compared with a baseline system that simply leaves the Scottish Gaelic source text unchanged, yielding a WER of 88.09%.

This is still not completely satisfactory as an evaluation for a couple of reasons. First, given the nature of the statistical model, the translations produced by `gd2ga` stay very close to the source language text, and so a sentence like

> *Tha mi a' tuigsinn a-nis.*
> ("I understand now.")

translates to

> *Tá mé ag tuiscint anois.*

whereas a human translator might render this more naturally in Irish as "*Tuigim anois.*". Similar examples in other verb tenses abound. Secondly, the system sometimes gets initial mutations wrong (tending to be conservative and preserving the mutations of the source text due to the penalty factor β), though this rarely impacts comprehension or fidelity of the translation. It might be reasonable to compute a modified WER for Celtic languages that ignores differences in mutations, but we did not pursue this.

4 Irish Standardizer

The standardizer described in this section takes as input an Irish language text and outputs a version that conforms as closely as possible to "standard Irish", subject to the vagaries discussed above in section 2.1. The principal application of the standardizer has been to the indexing of pre-standard texts to enable search and retrieval via standard spellings, mainly for lexicographical purposes (Uí Dhonnchadha et al., 2014). In this application, the standardized texts are used only for indexing purposes, which is to say that the pre-standard texts are displayed to users in search results.

An interesting second application would be to apply the standardizer to the huge amount of Irish language literature (novels, plays, many of them in translation) published from the 1920's through the 1940's in order to make those texts accessible to a modern readership that has grown up on the standard orthography. Indeed, a number of these books have been republished in recent years, but to my knowledge they have all been standardized by hand, e.g. (Doyle, 2012). To do this automatically, somewhat more care would be needed in order to not completely destroy the richness of the Irish dialects found in these texts (as the standardizer in its current form does, more or less), probably by creating customized versions of the standardizer for each dialect, together with limited post-editing.

4.1 Parallel Corpus

To support development of the "bilingual" lexicon (pre-standard/standard word pairs) and spelling rules, and to enable formal evaluation of the system, we created a large parallel corpus of pre-standard/standard sentence pairs. The standardizations were taken from republications of older material of the kind described above, and were performed manually by human editors. In all, we used eighteen books together with their standardizations, segmented by sentences and aligned into 46,914 translation pairs (almost all one sentence to one sentence). There are 814,365 words on the pre-standard side and 801,236 words on the standard side.

4.2 Lexicography

The bilingual lexicon is similar in structure to the Scottish Gaelic–Irish lexicon described above in section 3.2, with pre-standard lemmas being mapped to standard lemmas, and morphological generators applied to each side to create mappings of surface forms. The lexicon again draws upon existing resources; first and foremost, about 22,000 standardization pairs used by *An Gramadóir* for spelling and grammar correction, along with an additional 10,000 pairs drawn directly from an electronic version of (Ó Dónaill, 1977). After applying the morphological generators, we end up with mappings for about 135,000 surface forms. Keep in mind, however, that the spelling rules play a more important role for the standardizer than they do for the Scottish Gaelic translator, and so the actual source language coverage on pre-standard Irish texts is significantly better than the number 135,000 might suggest.

4.3 Evaluation

We performed two evaluations of the standardizer.

The first evaluation is similar to the one we performed on `gd2ga`, described above in section 3.3. Namely, we held out a sample of 200 sentence pairs from the parallel corpus, applied the standardizer to the pre-standard sentences, and compared the results with the reference standardizations, yielding a WER of 9.86%. Of course the translation problem here is much easier, as illustrated by a baseline WER of 27.28% obtained by leaving the pre-standard texts unchanged.

System	WER	Baseline
`gd2ga`	38.67	88.09
Standardizer	9.86	27.28

Table 1: Summary of results (Word Error Rates)

As a second evaluation, we looked at *sentence-level* accurancy. The point here is that in most cases there really is one "optimal" standardization of a given input sentence and that should be our aim. For example, the pre-standard

> *Acht go h-ádhmhail bhí lucht síothchána thall agus i bhfos.*
> ("But, luckily, there were peaceful people on both sides.")

must, in a just world, map to:

> *Ach go hádhúil bhí lucht síochána thall agus abhus.*

and we would consider any other standardization as incorrect.

The second evaluation, therefore, involves holding out a sample of 4147 sentence pairs from the parallel corpus, applying the standardizer to the pre-standard sentences, and comparing word-for-word with the standardized sentence (ignoring differences in punctuation). The current version gets 35.06% of these sentences completely correct. This can be compared with a score of 7.45% for a baseline system that does nothing to the input text (that is, 7.45% of the pre-standard sentences require no standardization at all, mostly very short sentences).

Acknowledgements

First and foremost I would like to thank Michael Bauer for making all of his Scottish Gaelic resources freely available, and for his outstanding work translating open-source software packages into Scottish

Gaelic. When combined with my own translations into Irish, these make up fully half of the Irish–Scottish Gaelic parallel corpus. Thanks also to Caoimhín Ó Donnaíle for providing access to a wealth of Scottish Gaelic lexicographical material and for answering many linguistic questions over the years. Donncha King kindly provided copies of several hard-to-find Irish translations of Scottish Gaelic short stories, along with the originals. I am grateful also to Ciarán Ó Duibhín for a number of useful email conversations regarding Irish standardization. The teams from the New English-Irish dictionary project and the Royal Irish Academy's *Foclóir na Nua-Ghaeilge*, especially Pádraig Ó Mianáin, Cathal Convery, Ruairí Ó hUiginn, and Máire Nic Mhaoláin, manually corrected the output of early versions of the standardizer which greatly sped up development. Finally, thanks to Elaine Uí Dhonnchadha and Brian Ó Raghallaigh for bravely installing and running unwieldly versions of the standardizer. This work was partially supported by US NSF grant 1159174.

References

Kemal Altintas and Ilyas Cicekli. 2002. A Machine Translation System Between a Pair of Closely Related Languages. In *Proceedings of the International Symposium on Computer and Information Sciences*, 192–196.

Michael Bauer. 2014. *Am Faclair Beag: Faclair Gáidhlig is Beurla le Dwelly 'na bhroinn [An English–Scottish Gaelic dictionary incorporating Dwelly]* `http://www.faclair.com/`. Retrieved June 26, 2014.

Michael Bauer. 2014. Speech and Language Technology on a Shoestring and how to get there in a hurry. `http://www.akerbeltz.org/iGaidhlig/wp-content/uploads/2014/07/SALT-on-a-Shoestring.pdf`. Retrieved July 3, 2014.

Peter F. Brown, Vincent J. Della Pietra, Stephen A. Della Pietra, and Robert L. Mercer. 1993. The mathematics of statistical machine translation: parameter estimation. *Computational Linguistics*, 19(2):263–311.

Stanley F. Chen and Joshua Goodman. 1996. An empirical study of smoothing techniques for language modeling. In *ACL '96 Proceedings of the 34th annual meeting on Association for Computational Linguistics*, 310–318.

Antonio M. Corbí-Bellot, Mikel L. Forcada, Sergio Ortiz-Rojas, Juan Antonio Pérez, Gema Ramírez-Sánchez, Felipe Sánchez-Martínez, Iñaki Alegria, and Kepa Sarasola. 2005. An Open-Source Shallow-Transfer Machine Translation Engine for the Romance Languages of Spain. In *Proceedings of the 10th European Assocaitation for Machine Translation Conference*, 79–86.

Tomás de Bhaldraithe. 1959. *English–Irish Dictionary*. Oifig an tSoláthair, Baile Átha Cliath.

Niall Ó Dónaill. 1977. *Foclóir Gaeilge-Béarla [Irish–English Dictionary]*. Oifig an tSoláthair, Baile Átha Cliath.

Elaine Uí Dhonnchadha, Kevin Scannell, Ruairí Ó hUiginn, Eilís Ní Mhearraí, Máire Nic Mhaoláin, Brian Ó Raghallaigh, Gregory Toner, Séamus Mac Mathúna, Déirdre D'Auria, Eithne Ní Ghallchobhair, and Niall O'Leary. 2014. Corpas na Gaeilge (1882-1926): Integrating Historical and Modern Irish Texts. *Proceedings of the Workshop "Language resources and technologies for processing and linking historical documents and archives" at LREC 2014.*

Arthur Conan Doyle. 2012. *Cú na mBaskerville [The Hound of the Baskervilles]*. Translated by Nioclás Tóibín, standardized by Aibhistín Ó Duibh. Evertype, Co. Mhaigh Eo.

Vivian Uíbh Eachach, ed. 2012. *Gramadach na Gaeilge: An Caighdeán Oifigiúil, Caighdeán Athbhreithnithe [Irish Grammar: The Official Standard, Revised Standard]*. `http://www.oireachtas.ie/parliament/media/Final-Version.pdf`. Seirbhísí Thithe an Oireachtais, Baile Átha Cliath.

Mikel L. Forcada, Mireia Ginestí-Rosell, Jacob Nordfalk, Jim O'Regan, Sergio Ortiz-Rojas, Juan Antonio Pérez-Ortiz, Felipe Sánchez-Martínez, Gema Ramírez-Sánchez, and Francis M. Tyers. 2011. Apertium: a free/open-source platform for rule-based machine translation *Machine Translation*, 25(2):127–144.

Jan Hajič, Jan Hric, and Vladislav Kuboň. 2000. Machine translation of very close languages. In *ANLC '00 Proceedings of the sixth conference on Applied natural language processing*, 7–12.

John Judge, Ailbhe Ní Chasaide, Rose Ní Dhubhda, Elaine Uí Dhonnchadha, and Kevin Scannell. 2012. *An Ghaeilge sa Ré Dhigiteach [The Irish Language in the Digital Age]*. Springer-Verlag, Berlin.

Antain Mac Lochlainn. 2012. Léirmheas ar an Chaighdeán Oifigiúil, 2012 [Review of the Official Standard, 2012]. http://www.aistear.ie/news-details.php?ID=33. Retrieved May 2, 2014.

Bryce Miller. 2008. Translating Between Closely Related Languages in Statistical Machine Translation. MS Thesis, University of Edinburgh.

Preslav Nakov and Jörg Tiedemann. 2012. Combining word-level and character-level models for machine translation between closely-related languages. In *ACL '12 Proceedings of the 50th Annual Meeting of the Association for Computational Linguistics: Short Papers - Volume 2*, 301–305.

Eva Pettersson, Beáta Megyesi, and Jörg Tiedemann. 2013. An SMT Approach to Automatic Annotation of Historical Text. In *Proceedings of the Workshop on Computational Historical Linguistics at NODALIDA 2013, NEALT Proceedings Series 18; Linkping Electronic Conference Proceedings*, 54–69.

Rannóg an Aistriúcháin [The Translation Section]. 1945. *Litriú na Gaeilge: Lámhleabhar an Chaighdeáin Oifigiúil [Irish Spelling: Handbook of the Official Standard]*. Oifig an tSoláthair, Baile Átha Cliath.

Rannóg an Aistriúcháin [The Translation Section]. 1958. *Gramadach na Gaeilge agus Litriú na Gaeilge [Grammar of Irish and Spelling of Irish]*. Oifig an tSoláthair, Baile Átha Cliath.

Kevin P. Scannell. 2006. Machine translation for closely related language pairs. In *Proceedings of the Workshop "Strategies for developing machine translation for minority languages" at LREC 2006*, 103–107.

Kevin P. Scannell. 2007. The Crúbadán Project: Corpus building for under-resourced languages. In *Proceedings of the 3rd Web as Corpus Workshop (WAC3) in Louvain-la-Neuve, Belgium*, 5–15.

Kevin P. Scannell. 2013. Mapping the Celtic Twittersphere. http://indigenoustweets.blogspot.ie/2013/12/mapping-celtic-twittersphere.html. Retrieved May 2, 2014.

Scottish Qualifications Authority. 2009. *Gaelic Orthographic Conventions*. http://www.sqa.org.uk/sqa/files_ccc/SQA-Gaelic_Orthographic_Conventions-G-e.pdf Ughdarras Theisteanas na h-Alba, Glasgow.

Francis M. Tyers. 2009. Rule-based augmentation of training data in BretonFrench statistical machine translation. In *Proceedings of the 13th Annual Conference of the European Association of Machine Translation, EAMT09*.

Cross-lingual Transfer Parsing for Low-Resourced Languages: An Irish Case Study

Teresa Lynn[1,2], **Jennifer Foster**[1], **Mark Dras**[2] and **Lamia Tounsi**[1]
[1]CNGL, School of Computing, Dublin City University, Ireland
[2]Department of Computing, Macquarie University, Sydney, Australia
[1]{tlynn,jfoster,ltounsi}@computing.dcu.ie
[2]{teresa.lynn,mark.dras}@mq.edu.au

Abstract

We present a study of cross-lingual direct transfer parsing for the Irish language. Firstly we discuss mapping of the annotation scheme of the Irish Dependency Treebank to a universal dependency scheme. We explain our dependency label mapping choices and the structural changes required in the Irish Dependency Treebank. We then experiment with the universally annotated treebanks of ten languages from four language family groups to assess which languages are the most useful for cross-lingual parsing of Irish by using these treebanks to train delexicalised parsing models which are then applied to sentences from the Irish Dependency Treebank. The best results are achieved when using Indonesian, a language from the Austronesian language family.

1 Introduction

Considerable efforts have been made over the past decade to develop natural language processing resources for the Irish language (Uí Dhonnchadha et al., 2003; Uí Dhonnchadha and van Genabith, 2006; Uí Dhonnchadha, 2009; Lynn et al., 2012a; Lynn et al., 2012b; Lynn et al., 2013). One such resource is the Irish Dependency Treebank (Lynn et al., 2012a) which contains just over 1000 gold standard dependency parse trees. These trees are labelled with deep syntactic information, marking grammatical roles such as subject, object, modifier, and coordinator. While a valuable resource, the treebank does not compare in size to similar resources of other languages.[1] The small size of the treebank affects the accuracy of any statistical parsing models learned from this treebank. Therefore, we would like to investigate whether training data from other languages can be successfully utilised to improve Irish parsing.

Cross-lingual transfer parsing involves training a parser on one language, and parsing data of another language. McDonald et al. (2011) describe two types of cross-lingual parsing, direct transfer parsing in which a delexicalised version of the source language treebank is used to train a parsing model which is then used to parse the target language, and a more complicated projected transfer approach in which the direct transfer approach is used to seed a parsing model which is then trained to obey source-target constraints learned from a parallel corpus. These experiments revealed that languages that were typologically similar were not necessarily the best source-target pairs, sometimes due to variations between their language-specific annotation schemes. In more recent work, however, McDonald et al. (2013) reported improved results on cross-lingual direct transfer parsing using a universal annotation scheme, to which six chosen treebanks are mapped for uniformity purposes. Underlying the experiments with this new annotation scheme is the universal part-of-speech (POS) tagset designed by Petrov et al. (2012). While their results confirm that parsers trained on data from languages in the same language group (e.g. Romance and Germanic) show the most accurate results, they also show that training data taken across language-groups also produces promising results. We attempt to apply the direct transfer approach with Irish as the target language.

The Irish language belongs to the Celtic branch of the Indo-European language family. The natural first step in cross-lingual parsing for Irish would be to look to those languages of the Celtic language

[1]For example, the Danish dependency treebank has 5,540 trees (Kromann, 2003); the Finnish dependency treebank has 15,126 trees (Haverinen et al., 2013)

Proceedings of the First Celtic Language Technology Workshop, pages 41–49,
Dublin, Ireland, August 23 2014.

group, i.e. Welsh, Scots Gaelic, Manx, Breton and Cornish, as a source of training data. However, these languages are just as, if not further, under-resourced. Thus, we attempt to use the languages of the universal dependency treebanks (McDonald et al., 2013).

The paper is organised as follows. In Section 2, we give an overview of the status of the Irish language and the Irish Dependency Treebank. Section 3 describes the mapping of the Irish Dependency Treebank's POS tagset (Uí Dhonnchadha and van Genabith, 2006) to that of Petrov et al. (2012), and the Irish Dependency Treebank annotation scheme (Lynn et al. (2012b)) to the Universal Dependency Scheme. Following that, in Section 4 we carry out cross-lingual direct transfer parsing experiments with ten harmonised treebanks to assess whether any of these languages are suitable for such parsing transfer for Irish. Section 5 summarises our work.

2 Irish Language and Treebank

Irish, a minority EU language, is the national and official language of Ireland. Despite this status, Irish is only spoken on a daily basis by a minority. As a Celtic language, Irish shares specific linguistic features with other Celtic languages, such as a VSO (verb-subject-object) word order and interesting morphological features such as inflected prepositions and initial mutations, for example.

Compared to other EU-official languages, Irish language technology is under-resourced, as highlighted by a recent study (Judge et al., 2012). In the area of morpho-syntactic processing, recent years have seen the development of a part-of-speech tagger (Uí Dhonnchadha and van Genabith, 2006), a morphological analyser (Uí Dhonnchadha et al., 2003), a shallow chunker (Uí Dhonnchadha, 2009), a dependency treebank (Lynn et al., 2012a; Lynn et al., 2012b) and statistical dependency parsing models for MaltParser (Nivre et al., 2006) and Mate parser (Bohnet, 2010) trained on this treebank (Lynn et al., 2013).

The annotation scheme for the Irish Dependency Treebank (Lynn et al., 2012b) was inspired by Lexical Functional Grammar (Bresnan, 2001) and has its roots in the dependency annotation scheme described by Çetinoğlu et al. (2010). It was extended and adapted to suit the linguistic characterisics of the Irish language. The final label set consists of 47 dependency labels, defining grammatical and functional relations between the words in a sentence. The label set is hierarchical in nature with labels such as `vparticle` (verb particle) and `vocparticle` (vocative particle), for example, representing more fine-grained versions of the `particle` label.

3 A universal dependency scheme for the Irish Dependency Treebank

In this section, we describe how a "universal" version of the Irish Dependency Treebank was created by mapping the original POS tags to universal POS tags and mapping the original dependency scheme to the universal dependency scheme. The result of this effort is an alternative version of the Irish Dependency Treebank which will be made available to the research community along with the original.

3.1 Mapping the Irish POS tagset to the Universal POS tagset

The Universal POS tagset (Petrov et al., 2012) has been designed to facilitate unsupervised and cross-lingual part-of-speech tagging and parsing research, by simplifying POS tagsets and unifying them across languages. The Irish Dependency Treebank was built upon a POS-tagged corpus developed by Uí Dhonnchadha and van Genabith (2006). The treebank's tagset contains both coarse- and fine-grained POS tags which we map to the Universal POS tags (e.g. Prop Noun → NOUN). Table 1 shows the mappings.

Most of the POS mappings made from the Irish POS tagset to the universal tagset are intuitive. However, some decisions require explanation.

Cop → VERB There are two verbs 'to be' in Irish: the substantive verb *bí* and the copula *is*. For that reason, the Irish POS tagset differentiates the copula by using the POS tag `Cop`. In Irish syntax literature, there is some discussion over its syntactic role, whether it is a verb or a linking particle. The role normally played is that of a linking element between a subject and a predicate. However, Lynn et al. (2012a)'s syntactic analysis of the copula is in line with that of Stenson (1981), regarding it as a verb. In addition, because the copula is often labelled in the Irish annotation scheme as the syntactic head of the matrix clause, we have chosen `VERB` as the most suitable mapping for this part of speech.

Part-of-speech (POS) mappings			
Universal	**Irish**	**Universal**	**Irish**
NOUN	Noun Noun, Pron Ref, Subst Subst, Verbal Noun, Prop Noun	ADP	Prep Deg, Prep Det, Prep Pron, Prep Simp, Prep Poss, Prep CmpdNoGen, Prep Cmpd, Prep Art, Pron Prep
PRON	Pron Pers, Pron Idf, Pron Q, Pron Dem	ADV	Adv Temp, Adv Loc, Adv Dir, Adv Q, Adv Its, Adv Gn
VERB	Cop Cop, Verb PastInd, Verb PresInd, Verb PresImp, Verb VI, Verb VT, Verb VTI, Verb PastImp, Verb Cond, Verb FutInd, Verb VD, Verb Imper	PRT	Part Vb, Part Sup, Part Inf, Part Pat, Part Voc, Part Ad, Part Deg, Part Comp, Part Rel, Part Num, Part Cp,
DET	Art Art, Det Det	NUM	Num Num
ADJ	Prop Adj, Verbal Adj, Adj Adj	X	Item Item, Abr Abr, CM CM, CU CU, CC CC, Unknown Unknown, Guess Abr, Itj Itj, Foreign Foreign,
CONJ	Conj Coord, Conj Subord	.	. . .. ? ? ! ! : : ? . Punct Punct

Table 1: Mapping of Irish Coarse and Fine-grained POS pairs (coarse fine) to Universal POS tagset.

Pron Prep → ADP *Pron Prep* is the Irish POS tag for pronominal prepositions, which are also referred to as prepositional pronouns. Characteristic of Celtic languages, they are prepositions inflected with their pronominal objects – compare, for example, ***le** mo chara* 'with my friend' with ***leis*** 'with him'. While the Irish POS labelling scheme labels them as pronouns in the first instance, our dependency labelling scheme treats the relationship between them and their syntactic heads as `obl` (obliques) or `padjunct` (prepositional adjuncts). Therefore, we map them to `ADP` (adpositions).

3.2 Mapping the Irish Dependency Scheme to the Universal Dependency Scheme

The departure point for the design of the Universal Dependency Annotation Scheme (McDonald et al., 2013) was the Stanford typed dependency scheme (de Marneffe and Manning, 2008), which was adapted based on a cross-lingual analysis of six languages: English, French, German, Korean, Spanish and Swedish. Existing English and Swedish treebanks were automatically mapped to the new universal scheme. The rest of the treebanks were developed manually to ensure consistency in annotation. The study also reports some structural changes (e.g. Swedish treebank coordination structures). [2]

There are 41 dependency relation labels to choose from in the universal annotation scheme[3]. McDonald et al. (2013) use all labels in the annotation of the German and English treebanks. The remaining languages use varying subsets of the label set. In our study we map the Irish dependency annotation scheme to 30 of the universal labels. The mappings are given in Table 2.

As with the POS mapping discussed in Section 3.1, mapping the Irish dependency scheme to the universal scheme was relatively straightforward, due in part, perhaps, to a similar level of granularity suggested by the similar label set sizes (Irish 47; standard universal 41). That said, there were significant considerations made in the mapping process, which involved some structural change in the treebank and the introduction of more specific analyses in the labelling scheme. These are discussed below.

3.2.1 Structural Differences

The following structural changes were made manually before the dependency labels were mapped to the universal scheme.

coordination The most significant structural change made to the treebank was an adjustment to the analysis of coordination. The original Irish Dependency Treebank subscribes to the LFG coordination analysis, where the coordinating conjunction (e.g. *agus* 'and') is the head, with the coordinates as its dependents, labelled `coord` (see Figure 1). The Universal Dependency Annotation scheme, on the

[2]There are two versions of the annotation scheme: the *standard* version (where copulas and adpositions are syntactic heads), and the *content-head* version which treats content words as syntactic heads. We are using the *standard* version for our study.

[3]The `vmod` label is used only in the content-head version.

Dependency Label Mappings			
Universal	**Irish**	**Universal**	**Irish**
root	top	*csubj*	csubj
acomp	adjpred, advpred, ppred	*dep*	for
adpcomp	N/A	*det*	det, det2, dem
adpmod	padjunct, obl, obl2, obl_ag	*dobj*	obj, vnobj, obj_q
adpobj	pobj	*mark*	subadjunct
advcl	N/A	*nmod*	addr, nadjunct
advmod	adjunct, advadjunct, quant, advadjunct_q	*nsubj*	subj, subj_q
amod	adjadjunct	*num*	N/A
appos	app	*p*	punctuation
attr	npred	*parataxis*	N/A
aux	toinfinitive	*poss*	poss
cc	N/A	*prt*	particle, vparticle, nparticle, advparticle, vocparticle, particlehead, cleftparticle, qparticle, aug
ccomp	comp	*rcmod*	relmod
compmod	nadjunct	*rel*	relparticle
conj	coord	*xcomp*	xcomp

Table 2: Mapping of Irish Dependency Annotation Scheme to Universal Dependency Annotation Scheme

other hand, uses right-adjunction, where the first coordinate is the head of the coordination, and the rest of the phrase is adjoined to the right, labelling coordinating conjunctions as `cc` and the following coordinates as `conj` (Figure 2).

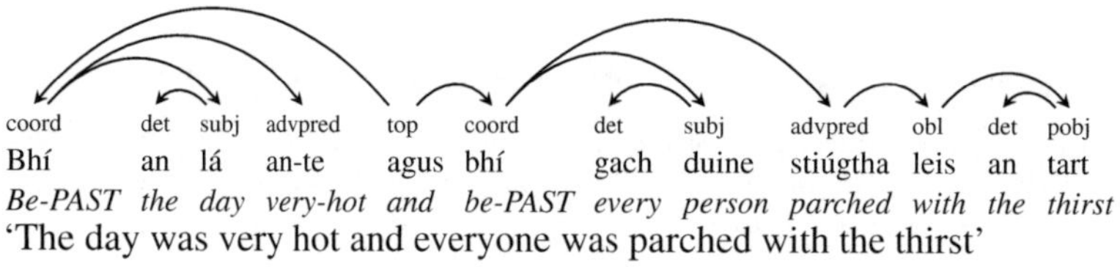

Figure 1: LFG-style coordination of original Irish Dependency Treebank

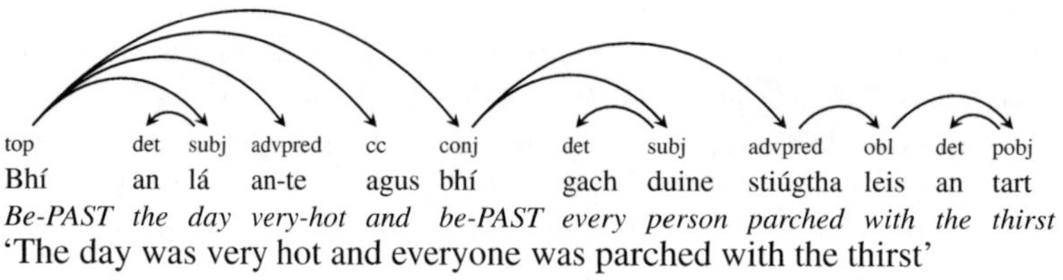

Figure 2: Stanford-style coordination changes to original Irish Dependency Treebank

subordinate clauses In the original Irish Dependency Treebank, the link between a matrix clause and its subordinate clause is similar to that of LFG: the subordinating conjunction (e.g. *mar* 'because', *nuair* 'when') is a `subadjunct` dependent of the matrix verb, and the head of the subordinate clause is a `comp` dependent of the subordinating conjunction (Figure 3). In contrast, the universal scheme is in line with the Stanford analysis of subordinate clauses, where the head of the clause is dependent on the matrix verb, and the subordinating conjunction is a dependent of the clause head (Figure 4).

3.2.2 Differences between dependency types

We found that the original Irish scheme makes distinctions that the universal scheme does not – this finer-grained information takes the form of the following Irish-specific dependency types: `advpred`,

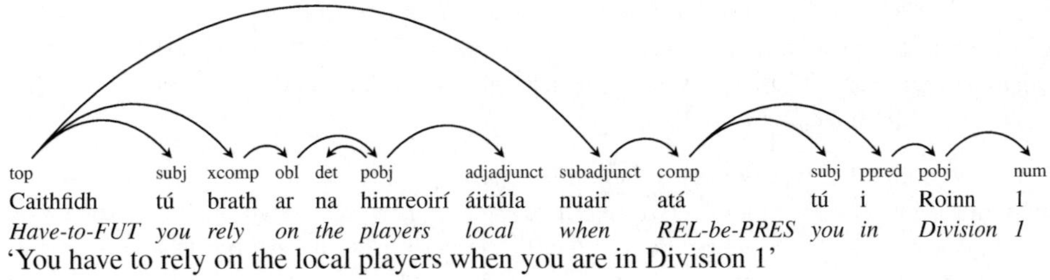

Figure 3: LFG-style subordinate clause analysis (with original Irish Dependency labels)

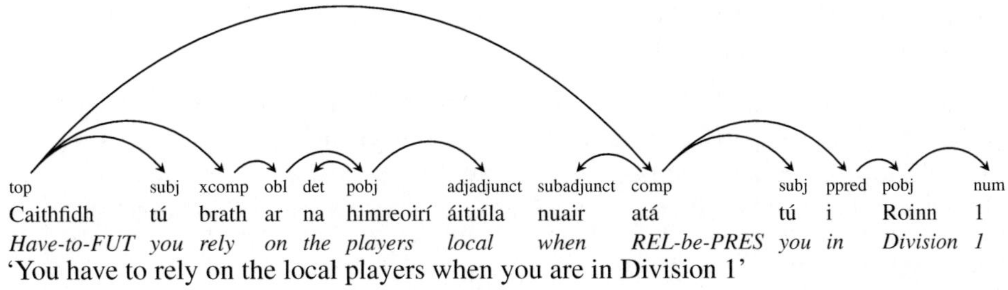

Figure 4: Stanford-style subordinate clause analysis (with original Irish Dependency labels)

`ppred`, `subj_q`, `obj_q`, `advadjunct_q`, `obl`, `obl2`. In producing the universal version of the treebank, these Irish-specific dependency types are mapped to less informative universal ones (see Table 2). Conversely, we found that the universal scheme makes distinctions that the Irish scheme does not. Some of these dependency types are not needed for Irish. For example, there is no indirect object `iobj` in Irish, nor is there a passive construction that would require `nsubjpass`, `csubjpass` or `auxpass`. Also, in the Irish Dependency Treebank, the copula is usually the root (`top`) or the head of a subordinate clause (e.g. `comp`) which renders the universal type `cop` redundant. Others that are not used are `adp`, `expl`, `infmod`, `mwe`, `neg`, `partmod`. However, we did identify some dependency relationships in the universal scheme that we introduce to the universal Irish Dependency Treebank (`adpcomp, adposition, advcl, num, parataxis`). These are explained below.

comp → adpcomp, advcl, parataxis, ccomp The following new mappings were previously subsumed by the Irish dependency label `comp` (complement clause). The mapping for *comp* has thus been split between *adpcomp*, *advcl*, *parataxis* and *ccomp*.

- `adpcomp` is a clausal complement of an adposition. An example from the English data is "some understanding of what the company's long-term horizon should **begin** to look like", where 'begin', as the head of the clause, is a dependent of the preposition 'of'. An example of how we use this label in Irish is: *an líne lántosach is mó clú a tháinig as Ciarraí ó* ***bhí*** *aimsir Sheehy ann* 'the most renowned forward line to come out of Kerry since Sheehy's time' (lit. 'from it was Sheehy's time'). The verb *bhí* 'was', head of the dependent clause, is an `adcomp` dependent of the preposition *ó*.

- `advcl` is used to identify adverbial clause modifiers. In the English data, they are often introduced by subordinating conjunctions such as 'when', 'because', 'although', 'after', 'however', etc. An example is "However, because the guaranteed circulation base is being **lowered**, ad rates will be higher". Here, 'lowered' is a `advcl` dependent of 'will'. An example of usage is: *Tá truailliú mór san áit mar nach* ***bhfuil*** *córas séarachais ann* 'There is a lot of pollution in the area because there **is** no sewerage system', where *bhfuil* 'is' is an `advcl` dependent of *Tá* 'is'.

- parataxis labels clausal structures that are separated from the previous clause with punctuation such as – ... : () ; and so on. Examples in Irish *Is léir go bhfuil ag éirí le feachtas an IDA – **meastar** gur in Éirinn a lonnaítear timpeall 30% de na hionaid* 'It is clear that the IDA campaign is succeeding – it **is believed** that 30% of the centres are based in Ireland'. Here, *meastar* 'is believed' is a parataxis dependent of *Is* 'is'.

- ccomp covers all other types of clausal complements. For example, in English, 'Mr. Amos says the Show-Crier team will probably **do** two live interviews a day'. The head of the complement clause here is 'do', which is a comp dependent of the matrix verb 'says'. A similar Irish example is: *Dúirt siad nach **bhfeiceann** siad an cineál seo chomh minic* 'They said that they don't **see** this type as often'. Here, *bhfeiceann* 'see' is the head of the complement clause, which is a comp dependent of the verb *Dúirt* 'Said'.

quant → num, advmod The Irish Dependency Scheme uses one dependency label (quant) to cover all types of numerals and quantifiers. We now use the universal scheme to differentiate between quantifiers such as *mórán* 'many' and numerals such as *fiche* 'twenty'.

nadjunct → nmod, compmod The Irish dependency label nadjunct accounts for all nominal modifiers. However, in order to map to the universal scheme, we discriminate two kinds: (i) nouns that modify nouns (usually genitive case in Irish) are mapped to compmod (e.g. *plean **margaíochta*** '**marketing** plan') and (ii) nouns that modify clauses are mapped to nmod (e.g. ***bliain** ó shin* 'a **year** ago').

4 Parsing Experiments

We now describe how we extend the direct transfer experiments described in McDonald et al. (2013) to Irish. In Section 4.1, we describe the datasets used in our experiments and explain the experimental design. In Section 4.2, we present the results, which we then discuss in Section 4.3.

4.1 Data and Experimental Setup

We present the datasets used in our experiments and explain how they are used. Irish is the target language for all our parsing experiments.

Universal Irish Dependency Treebank This is the universal version of the Irish Dependency Treebank which contains 1020 gold-standard trees, which have been mapped to the Universal POS tagset and Universal Dependency Annotation Scheme, as described in Section 3. In order to establish a monolingual baseline against which to compare our cross-lingual results, we perform a five-fold cross-validation by dividing the full data set into five non-overlapping training/test sets. We also test our cross-lingual models on an *delexicalised* version of this treebank.

Transfer source training data For our direct transfer cross-lingual parsing experiments, we use 10 of the standard version harmonised training data sets[4] made available by McDonald et al. (2013): Brazilian Portuguese (PT-BR), English (EN), French (FR), German (DE), Indonesian (ID), Italian (IT), Japanese (JA), Korean (KO), Spanish (ES) and Swedish (SV). For the purposes of uniformity, we select the first 4447 trees from each treebank – to match the number of trees in the smallest data set (Swedish). We delexicalise all treebanks and use the universal POS tags as both the coarse- and fine-grained values.[5] We train a parser on all 10 source data sets outlined and use each induced parsing model to parse and test on a *delexicalised* version of the Universal Irish Dependency Treebank.

Largest transfer source training data - Universal English Dependency Treebank English has the largest source training data set (sections 2-21 of the Wall Street Journal data in the Penn Treebank (Marcus et al., 1993) contains 39, 832 trees). As with the smaller transfer datasets, we delexicalise this dataset and use the universal POS tag values only. We experiment with this larger training set in order to establish whether more training data helps in a cross-lingual setting.

[4]Version 2 data sets downloaded from https://code.google.com/p/uni-dep-tb/

[5]Note that the downloaded treebanks had some fine-grained POS tags that were not used across all languages: e.g. VERB-VPRT (Spanish), CD (English).

Parser and Evaluation Metrics We use a transition-based dependency parsing system, MaltParser (Nivre et al., 2006) for all of our experiments. All our models are trained using the stacklazy algorithm, which can handle the non-projective trees present in the Irish data. In each case we report Labelled Attachment Score (LAS) and Unlabelled Attachment Score (UAS).[6]

4.2 Results

All cross-lingual results are presented in Table 3. Note that when we train and test on Irish (our monolingual baseline), we achieve an average accuracy of 78.54% (UAS) and 71.59% (LAS) over the five cross-validation runs. The cross-lingual results are substantially lower than this baseline. The LAS results range from 0.84 (JA) to 43.88 (ID) and the UAS from 16.74 (JA) to 61.69 (ID).

	SingleT										*MultiT*	*LargestT*
Training	EN	FR	DE	ID	IT	JA	KO	PT-BR	ES	SV	All	EN
UAS	51.72	56.84	49.21	**61.69**	50.98	16.74	18.02	57.31	57.00	49.95	57.69	51.59
LAS	35.03	37.91	33.04	**43.88**	37.98	0.84	9.35	42.13	41.94	34.02	41.38	33.97
Experiment	*SingleT-30*										*MultiT-30*	*LargestT-30*
Training	EN	FR	DE	ID	IT	JA	KO	PT-BR	ES	SV	All	EN
Avg sent len	23	24	16	21	21	9	11	24	26	14	19	23
UAS	55.97	60.98	53.42	**64.86**	54.47	16.88	19.27	60.47	60.53	54.40	61.40	55.54
LAS	38.42	41.44	36.24	**46.45**	40.56	1.19	10.08	45.04	45.23	37.76	44.63	37.08

Table 3: Multi-lingual transfer parsing results

A closer look at the single-source transfer parsing evaluation results (*SingleT*) shows that some language sources are particularly strong for parsing accuracy of certain labels. For example, `ROOT` (for Indonesian), `adpobj` (for French) and `amod` (for Spanish). In response to these varied results, we explore the possibility of combining the strengths of all the source languages (*multi-source direct transfer* (*MultiT*) – also implemented by McDonald et al. (2011)). A parser is trained on a concatenation of all the delexicalised source data described in Section 4.1 and tested on the full delexicalised Universal Irish Dependency Treebank. Combining all source data produces parsing results of 57.69% (UAS) and 41.38% (LAS), which is outperformed by the best individual source language model.

Parsing with the large English training set (*LargestT*) yielded results of 51.59 (UAS) and 33.97 (LAS) compared to a UAS/LAS of 51.72/35.05 for the smaller English training set. We investigated more closely why the larger training set did not improve performance by incrementally adding training sentences to the smaller set – none of these increments reveal any higher scores, suggesting that English is not a suitable source training language for Irish.

It is well known that sentence length has a negative effect on parsing accuracy. As noted in earlier experiments (Lynn et al., 2012b), the Irish Dependency Treebank contains some very long difficult-to-parse sentences (some legal text exceeds 300 tokens in length). The average sentence length is 27 tokens. By placing a 30-token limit on the Universal Irish Dependency Treebank we are left with 778 sentences, with an average sentence length of 14. We use this new 30-token-limit version of the Irish Dependency Treebank data to test our parsing models. The results are shown in the lower half of Table 3. Not surprisingly, the results rise substantially for all models.

4.3 Discussion

McDonald et al. (2013)'s single-source transfer parsing results show that languages within the same language groups make good source-target pairs. They also show reasonable accuracy of source-target pairing across language groups. For instance, the baseline when parsing French is 81.44 (UAS) and 73.37 (LAS), while the transfer results obtained using an English treebank are 70.14 (UAS) and 58.20(LAS). Our baseline parser for Irish yields results of 78.54 (UAS) and 71.59 (LAS), while Indonesian-Irish transfer results are 61.69 (UAS) and 43.88 (LAS).

The lowest scoring source language is Japanese. This parsing model's output shows less than 3% accuracy when identifying the `ROOT` label. This suggests the effect that the divergent word orders have

[6] All scores are micro-averaged.

on this type of cross-lingual parsing – VSO (Irish) vs SOV (Japanese). Another factor that is likely to be playing a role is the size of the Japanese sentences. The average sentence length in the Japanese training data is only 9 words, which means that this dataset is comparatively smaller than the others. It is also worth noting that the universal Japanese treebank uses only 15 of the 41 universal labels (the universal Irish treebank uses 30 of these labels).

As our best performing model (Indonesian) is an Austronesian language, we investigate why this language does better when compared to Indo-European languages. We compare the results obtained by the Indonesian parser with those of the English parser (*SingleT*). Firstly, we note that the Indonesian parser captures nominal modification much better than English, resulting in an increased precision-recall score of 60/67 on `compmod`. This highlights that the similarities in noun-noun modification between Irish and Indonesian helps cross-lingual parsing. In both languages the modifying noun directly follows the head noun, e.g. 'the statue of the hero' translates in Irish as *dealbh an laoich* (lit. statue the hero); in Indonesian as *patung palawan* (lit. statue hero). Secondly, our analysis shows that the English parser does not capture long-distance dependencies as well as the Indonesian parser. For example, we have observed an increased difference in precision-recall of 44%-44% on `mark`, 12%-17.88% on `cc` and 4%-23.17% on `rcmod` when training on Indonesian. Similar differences have also been observed when we compare with the French and English (*LargestT*) parsers. The Irish language allows for the use of multiple conjoined structures within a sentence and it appears that long-distance dependencies can affect cross-lingual parsing. Indeed, excluding very long sentences from the test set reveals substantial increases in precision-recall scores for labels such as `advcl`, `cc`, `conj` and `ccomp` – all of which are labels associated with long-distance dependencies.

With this study, we had hoped that we would be able to identify a way to bootstrap the development of the Irish Dependency Treebank and parser through the use of delexicalised treebanks annotated with the Universal Annotation Scheme. While the current treebank data might capture certain linguistic phenomena well, we expected that some cross-linguistic regularities could be taken advantage of. Although the best cross-lingual model failed to outperform the monolingual model, perhaps it might be possible to combine the strengths of the Indonesian and Irish treebanks? We performed 5-fold cross-validation on the combined Indonesian and Irish data sets. The results did not improve over the Irish model. We then analysed the extent of their complementarity by counting the number of sentences where the Indonesian model outperformed the Irish model. This happened in only 20 cases, suggesting that there is no benefit in using the Indonesian data over the Irish data nor in combining them at the sentence-level.

5 Conclusion and Future Work

In this paper, we have reported an implementation of cross-lingual direct transfer parsing of the Irish language. We have also presented and explained our mapping of the Irish Dependency Treebank to the Universal POS tagset and Universal Annotation Scheme. Our parsing results show that an Austronesian language surpasses Indo-European languages as source data for cross-lingual Irish parsing.

In extending this research, there are many interesting avenues which could be explored including the use of Irish as a source language for another Celtic language and experimenting with the projected transfer approach of McDonald et al. (2011).

Acknowledgements

This research is supported by the Science Foundation Ireland (Grant 12/CE/I2267) as part of the CNGL (www.cngl.ie) at Dublin City University. We thank the three anonymous reviewers for their helpful feedback. We also thank Elaine Uí Dhonnchadha (Trinity College Dublin) and Brian Ó Raghallaigh (Fiontar, Dublin City University) for their linguistic advice.

References

Bernd Bohnet. 2010. Top accuracy and fast dependency parsing is not a contradiction. In *Proceedings of COLING'10*.

Joan Bresnan. 2001. *Lexical Functional Syntax*. Oxford: Blackwell.

Özlem Çetinoğlu, Jennifer Foster, Joakim Nivre, Deirdre Hogan, Aoife Cahill, and Josef van Genabith. 2010. LFG without C-structures. In *Proceedings of the 9th International Workshop on Treebanks and Linguistic Theories*.

Marie-Catherine de Marneffe and Christopher D. Manning. 2008. The Stanford typed dependencies representation. In *Workshop on Crossframework and Cross-domain Parser Evaluation (COLING2008)*.

Katri Haverinen, Jenna Nyblom, Timo Viljanen, Veronika Laippala, Samuel Kohonen, Anna Missilä, Stina Ojala, Tapio Salakoski, and Filip Ginter. 2013. Building the essential resources for Finnish: the Turku dependency treebank. *Language Resources and Evaluation*, pages 1–39.

John Judge, Ailbhe Ní Chasaide, Rose Ní Dhubhda, Kevin P. Scannell, and Elaine Uí Dhonnchadha. 2012. *The Irish Language in the Digital Age*. Springer Publishing Company, Incorporated.

Matthias Kromann. 2003. The Danish Dependency Treebank and the DTAG Treebank Tool. In *Proceedings of the Second Workshop on Treebanks and Linguistic Theories (TLT2003)*.

Teresa Lynn, Özlem Çetinoğlu, Jennifer Foster, Elaine Uí Dhonnchadha, Mark Dras, and Josef van Genabith. 2012a. Irish treebanking and parsing: A preliminary evaluation. In *Proceedings of the Eight International Conference on Language Resources and Evaluation (LREC'12)*, pages 1939–1946.

Teresa Lynn, Jennifer Foster, Mark Dras, and Elaine Uí Dhonnchadha. 2012b. Active learning and the Irish treebank. In *Proceedings of the Australasian Language Technology Workshop (ALTA)*, pages 23–32.

Teresa Lynn, Jennifer Foster, and Mark Dras. 2013. Working with a small dataset – semi-supervised dependency parsing for Irish. In *Proceedings of the Fourth Workshop on Statistical Parsing of Morphologically-Rich Languages*, pages 1–11, Seattle, Washington, USA, October. Association for Computational Linguistics.

Mitchell P. Marcus, Beatrice Santorini, and Mary Ann Marcinkiewicz. 1993. Building a large annotated corpus of english: The Penn treebank. *COMPUTATIONAL LINGUISTICS*, 19(2):313–330.

Ryan McDonald, Slav Petrov, and Keith Hall. 2011. Multi-source transfer of delexicalized dependency parsers. In *Proceedings of the Conference on Empirical Methods in Natural Language Processing*, EMNLP '11, pages 62–72, Stroudsburg, PA, USA. Association for Computational Linguistics.

Ryan McDonald, Joakim Nivre, Yvonne Quirmbach-brundage, Yoav Goldberg, Dipanjan Das, Kuzman Ganchev, Keith Hall, Slav Petrov, Hao Zhang, Oscar Täckström, Claudia Bedini, Núria Bertomeu, and Castelló Jungmee Lee. 2013. Universal dependency annotation for multilingual parsing. In *Proceedings of ACL '13*.

Joakim Nivre, Johan Hall, and Jens Nilsson. 2006. Maltparser: A data-driven parser-generator for dependency parsing. In *Proceedings of the Fifth International Conference on Language Resources and Evaluation (LREC2006)*.

Slav Petrov, Dipanjan Das, and Ryan McDonald. 2012. A universal part-of-speech tagset. In *Proceedings of the Eight International Conference on Language Resources and Evaluation (LREC'12)*.

Nancy Stenson. 1981. *Studies in Irish Syntax*. Tübingen: Gunter Narr Verlag.

Elaine Uí Dhonnchadha and Josef van Genabith. 2006. A part-of-speech tagger for Irish using finite-state morphology and constraint grammar disambiguation. In *Proceedings of the 5th International Conference on Language Resources and Evaluation (LREC 2006)*.

Elaine Uí Dhonnchadha, Caoilfhionn Nic Pháidín, and Josef van Genabith. 2003. Design, implementation and evaluation of an inflectional morphology finite state transducer for Irish. *Machine Translation*, 18:173–193.

Elaine Uí Dhonnchadha. 2009. *Part-of-Speech Tagging and Partial Parsing for Irish using Finite-State Transducers and Constraint Grammar*. Ph.D. thesis, Dublin City University.

Irish National Morphology Database: a high-accuracy open-source dataset of Irish words

Michal Boleslav Měchura
New English-Irish Dictionary Project
Foras na Gaeilge
Dublin, Ireland
mmechura@forasnagaeilge.ie

Abstract

The Irish National Morphology Database is a human-verified, Official Standard-compliant dataset containing the inflected forms and other morpho-syntactic properties of Irish nouns, adjectives, verbs and prepositions. It is being developed by Foras na Gaeilge as part of the New English-Irish Dictionary project. This paper introduces this dataset and its accompanying software library *Gramadán*.

1 Introduction

The Irish National Morphology Database is a side product of the New English-Irish Dictionary project at Foras na Gaeilge. During work on the dictionary, a requirement arose to include rich morphological information on the target (Irish) side of the dictionary. It has been decided to build a separate morphological dataset that translations in the dictionary would link to. The result can be viewed at `http://focloir.ie/` where clicking a grammatical label next to a translation opens a window listing the inflected forms and other morphological properties of the word. The same data can also be viewed separately at `http://breis.focloir.ie/en/gram/`.

2 Database design

The Irish National Morphology Database has been compiled semi-automatically from several sources available to Foras na Gaeilge, including a machine-readable version of *Foclóir Póca* and grammatical data extracted from *WinGléacht* and *focal.ie*. All data resulting from this process have been proof-read and corrected by editors working on the New English-Irish Dictionary project. Therefore, we describe the database as a high-accuracy dataset: it does not come with a known margin of error and it is meant to have normative force. The language data complies with the Official Standard for Irish (*An Caighdeán Oifigiúil* 2012).

At time of writing, the database contains 6,736 nouns, 983 adjectives, 1,239 verbs and 16 prepositions. New entries are being added continuously.

Each entry has a unique identifier consisting of the lemma followed by a grammatical label, such as `bainis_fem2`. In cases where the grammatical label is not sufficient to distinguish between homonyms, the identifier contains a "disambiguator", such as `glúin_fem2_cos` (the noun *glúin* 'knee' with plural *glúine*) versus `glúin_fem2_aois` (the noun *glúin* 'generation' with plural *glúnta*). The disambiguators (*cos* 'leg', *aois* 'age') are purely mnemotechnic: no attempt is being made to expose the semantics of the lemmas, only that two different lemmas exist with two different sets of inflected forms.

The database structure allows for variation everywhere. Every inflected form (for example, every combination of case and number) is in essence a list of variants which can contain zero, one or more

Proceedings of the First Celtic Language Technology Workshop, pages 50–54,
Dublin, Ireland, August 23 2014.

forms, each with its own grammatical properties. Thus we can accommodate cases when the Offical Standard allows for variation, such as the two genitives of *talamh* 'land' (masculine *talaimh* and feminine *talún*). On the other hand, an empty list of variants implies the form does not exist (or is not known), for example when a noun has no plural.

The entries are encoded in XML. Every entry comes in two shapes: a **minimal** format which contains the smallest necessary set of forms and properties, and an **expanded** format intended for presentation to humans. For example, in the case of nouns, the minimal entries contain only one form for each number and case (e.g. *bainis* 'wedding' in singular nominative) while, in the expanded entry, these are "expanded" to include definitiveness (*bainis* 'a wedding', *an bhainis* 'the wedding'). The expanded entries are then transformed with XSL into HTML and displayed to human users. The minimal entries are intended as a machine-readable resource that can be re-used for other purposes in language technology, such as for building spellcheckers or for query expansion in fulltext search.

Minimal entries are converted into expanded entries using *Gramadán,* a custom-built software library written in C#. *Gramadán* provides functions for performing grammatical operations such as initial mutations, constructing noun phrases from nouns and adjectives, constructing verb phrases from verbs, and so on. The process of converting a minimal entry into an expanded entry is in essence an exercise in natural language generation (where syntactic structures are serialized into strings), and *Gramadán* is in essence a software library for natural language generation in Irish.

2.1 Nouns

Listing 1 shows a typical noun entry (*abhainn* 'river')[1] in minimal format, Listing 2 shows the same entry in expanded format. Notice that each form (`sgNom` being singular nominative, `sgGen` singular genitive and so on) consists of a string (the `default` attribute) with form-specific properties: singular forms have gender while plural forms do not, the plural genitive has strength (a property which signals whether the form is weak or strong). Notice that we have decided to treat gender as a property of a word form, not a property of the whole lemma. This makes it possible to deal with cases like *talamh* 'land' which has two singular genitives, one masculine and one feminine.

2.2 Adjectives

Listing 3 shows a typical adjective entry (*bán* 'white')[2] in minimal format, Listing 4 shows the same entry in expanded format. The forms of an adjective are less evenly distributed than those of a noun: there is one singular nominative, two singular genitives (for agreement with masculine and feminine nouns) and only one plural form for all cases (the singular nominative is used for agreement with weak-plural genitive nouns). This is sufficient information for *Gramadán* to generate the forms needed for agreement with all kinds of nouns in all numbers and cases, as can be seen in the expanded format. The minimal format also contains a graded form which is used by *Gramadán* to generate comparatives and superlatives in the past and present.

2.3 Verbs

Listing 5 shows an extract from a typical verb entry (*bagair* 'threaten')[3] in minimal format, Listing 6 shows a corresponding extract from the same entry in expanded format. Verbs are more complicated than nouns and adjectives in the sense that they contain many more forms. In the Irish National Morphology Database, a verb has forms for up to six **tenses** (past, past continuous, present, present continuous, future, conditional) and two **moods** (imperative, subjunctive). Note that we treat the conditional as a tense because it has the properties of a tense, even though grammar books traditionally categorize it as a mood.

The difference between a tense and a mood is that a tense can generate forms that are either declarative or interrogative, while a mood can only generate declarative forms (*bagair!* 'threaten!', *ná bagair!* 'don't threaten!'). Consequently, every tense form in the minimal format is labelled as being either **dependent** or **independent**, while mood forms have no such distinction. The dependent and independent forms are identical for many verbs, but different for some irregular ones (e.g. *déan* 'make'

1 For a user-friendly presentation of the noun, see `http://breis.focloir.ie/en/gram/abhainn`

2 For a user-friendly presentation of the adjective, see `http://breis.focloir.ie/en/gram/bán`

3 For a user-friendly presentation of the verb, see `http://breis.focloir.ie/en/gram/bagair`

in the past tense: independent *rinne*, dependent *dearna*). The independent forms generate positive declarative forms (*rinne mé* 'I made'), the dependent forms generate all others (*ní dhearna mé* 'I didn't make', *an ndearna mé?* 'did I make?', *nach ndearna mé?* 'didn't I make?')

Additionally, every tense and mood form is assigned to a **person,** which in our analysis is a conflation of person, number and other features: there is a "base" person from which analytic forms are generated (*rinne* 'made' → *rinne muid* 'we made'), there are singular/plural first/second/third persons for synthetic forms (*rinneamar* 'we made'), and there is an "autonomous" person for passive forms of the verb (*rinneadh* 'was made').

A typical verb has, in its minimal format, about 60 individual forms. This is the set from which *Gramadán* can generate a verb phrase in any tense or mood, person, number, polarity (positive or negative) and shape (declarative or interrogative). Unlike other parts of speech where the rules for generating an expanded entry from a minimal one are completely regular, the verbal component in *Gramadán* has some hard-coded exceptions for a small number of irregular verbs. Also, the verb *bí* 'be' is quite exceptional as it is the only verb that has both a present tense (*tá* 'is') and a continuous present tense (*bíonn* 'habitually is'); other verbs only have a continuous present tense (their non-continuous present tense is built analytically from the verbal noun). Finally, the Irish National Morphology Database does not include the copula *is*, as we do not think it is as a verb.

3 More about *Gramadán*

The tool used for processing data in the Irish National Morphology Database, *Gramadán*, deserves separate mention. Besides converting entries from minimal to expanded format, *Gramadán* has additional features both below and above the level of words.

Below the level of words, for nouns and adjectives that have not been included in the Irish National Morphology Database yet, *Gramadán* is able to derive their forms and properties from knowing which inflection class they belong to. Unlike the traditional inflection classes found in Irish dictionaries, *Gramadán* uses a radically different system, inspired by Carnie (2008), where singular and plural classes are separate.

Above the level of words, *Gramadán* can be used as a realisation engine in an NLG (natural language generation) setting. *Gramadán* is able to use data from the Irish National Morphology Database to construct noun phrases, prepositional phrases and rudimentary clauses while respecting the rules of gender and number agreement, initial mutations, case inflections and so on. This aspect of *Gramadán* is in development and the goal is, eventually, to cover all the basic syntactical phenomena of Irish including the construction of clauses containing the copula and the construction of numbered noun phrases (noun phrases with cardinal and ordinal numerals).

While many of *Gramadán's* features are used for processing the Irish National Morphology Database, it is an independent software tool which has potential applications beyond it.

4 Future plans

The Irish National Morphology Database is work in progress and will continue to be developed by Foras na Gaeilge along with other outputs from the New English-Irish Dictionary project. Once the database structure has been finalized and detailed documentation has been produced, the whole dataset (along with its accompanying tool, *Gramadán*) will be released under an open-source licence and made available for download on the Internet. In the longer term, we plan to develop the natural language generation aspect of *Gramadán* and to use it as a basis for assistive language technology, as well as to inform applied research into Irish morphosyntax.

References

An Caighdeán Oifigiúil [the Official Standard]. 2012. Houses of the Oireachtas, Dublin. `http://tinyurl.com/coif2012` (accessed 8 May 2014)

breis.foclóir.ie: Dictionary and Language Library. `http://beis.focloir.ie/`

Andrew Carnie. 2008. *Irish Nouns: A Reference Guide.* Oxford University Press, Oxford.

focal.ie: National Terminology Database for Irish. `http://www.focal.ie/`

foclóir.ie: New English-Irish Dictionary. http://www.focloir.ie/

Foclóir Póca, Irish-English/English-Irish dictionary. 1986. An Gúm and Department of Education, Dublin.

WinGléacht: CD-ROM. 2007. An Gúm, Dublin.

Appendix A. Code listings

Listing 1. The noun 'abhainn' in minimal format

```
<noun default="abhainn" declension="5" disambig="" isProper="0" isDefinite="0"
allowArticledGenitive="0">
 <sgNom default="abhainn" gender="fem"/>
 <sgGen default="abhann" gender="fem"/>
 <plNom default="aibhneacha"/>
 <plGen default="aibhneacha" strength="strong"/>
</noun>
```

Listing 2. The noun 'abhainn' in expanded format

```
<Lemma lemma="abhainn" uid="abhainn_fem5">
 <noun gender="fem" declension="5">
  <sgNom><articleNo>abhainn</articleNo><articleYes>an abhainn</articleYes></sgNom>
  <sgGen><articleNo>abhann</articleNo><articleYes>na habhann</articleYes></sgGen>
  <plNom><articleNo>aibhneacha</articleNo><articleYes>na haibhneacha</articleYes></plNom>
  <plGen><articleNo>aibhneacha</articleNo><articleYes>na n-aibhneacha</articleYes></plGen>
 </noun>
</Lemma>
```

Listing 3. The adjective 'bán' in minimal format

```
<adjective default="bán" declension="1" disambig="">
 <sgNom default="bán"/>
 <sgGenMasc default="báin"/><sgGenFem default="báine"/>
 <plNom default="bána"/>
 <graded default="báine"/>
</adjective>
```

Listing 4. The adjective 'bán' in expanded format

```
<Lemma lemma="bán" uid="bán_adj1">
 <adjective declension="1">
  <sgNomMasc>bán</sgNomMasc><sgNomFem>bhán</sgNomFem>
  <sgGenMasc>bháin</sgGenMasc><sgGenFem>báine</sgGenFem>
  <plNom>bána</plNom><plNomSlen>bhána</plNomSlen>
  <plGenStrong>bána</plGenStrong><plGenWeak>bán</plGenWeak>
  <comparPres>níos báine</comparPres><comparPast>ní ba bháine</comparPast>
  <superPres>is báine</superPres><superPast>ba bháine</superPast>
 </adjective>
</Lemma>
```

Listing 5. Extract from the verb 'bagair' in minimal format

```
<?xml version='1.0' encoding='utf-8'?>
<verb default="bagair" disambig="">
 <verbalNoun default="bagairt"/>
 <verbalAdjective default="bagartha"/>
 <tenseForm default="bagair" tense="Past" dependency="Indep" person="Base"/>
 <tenseForm default="bagraíomar" tense="Past" dependency="Indep" person="Pl1"/>
 <tenseForm default="bagraíodar" tense="Past" dependency="Indep" person="Pl3"/>
 <tenseForm default="bagraíodh" tense="Past" dependency="Indep" person="Auto"/>
 ...
</verb>
```

Listing 6. Extract from the verb 'bagair' in expanded format

```
<Lemma lemma="bagair" uid="bagair_verb">
 <verb>
  <vn>bagairt</vn>
  <va>bagartha</va>
  <past>
```

```
<sg1><pos>bhagair mé</pos><quest>ar bhagair mé?</quest><neg>níor bhagair mé</neg></sg1>
<sg2><pos>bhagair tú</pos><quest>ar bhagair tú?</quest><neg>níor bhagair tú</neg></sg2>
<sg3Masc><pos>bhagair sé</pos><quest>ar bhagair sé?</quest><neg>níor bhagair sé</neg></sg3Masc>
<sg3Fem><pos>bhagair sí</pos><quest>ar bhagair sí?</quest><neg>níor bhagair sí</neg></sg3Fem>
<pl1>
 <pos>bhagraíomar</pos><pos>bhagair muid</pos>
 <quest>ar bhagraíomar?</quest><quest>ar bhagair muid?</quest>
 <neg>níor bhagraíomar</neg><neg>níor bhagair muid</neg>
</pl1>
<pl2><pos>bhagair sibh</pos><quest>ar bhagair sibh?</quest><neg>níor bhagair sibh</neg></pl2>
<pl3>
 <pos>bhagair siad</pos><pos>bhagraíodar</pos>
 <quest>ar bhagair siad?</quest><quest>ar bhagraíodar?</quest>
 <neg>níor bhagair siad</neg><neg>níor bhagraíodar</neg>
</pl3>
<auto><pos>bagraíodh</pos><quest>ar bagraíodh?</quest><neg>níor bagraíodh</neg></auto>
</past>
...
</verb>
</Lemma>
```

Developing further speech recognition resources for Welsh

Sarah Cooper
Language Technologies Unit
Canolfan Bedwyr
Bangor University
s.cooper@bangor.ac.uk

Dewi Bryn Jones
Language Technologies Unit
Canolfan Bedwyr
Bangor University
d.b.jones@bangor.ac.uk

Delyth Prys
Language Technologies Unit
Canolfan Bedwyr
Bangor University
d.prys@bangor.ac.uk

Abstract

This paper reports on ongoing research into developing large-vocabulary continuous speech recognition (LVCSR) for the Welsh language. We address data design issues and the method for data collection using a purposely designed application for mobile devices. We also discuss the application of the data including the design and collection of a small speech corpus to cover the commands used to control a robotic arm in Welsh on a Raspberry Pi computer the licensing of the project and our hopes for the application of the project resources to other languages.

1 Introduction

This paper presents an overview of the GALLU (Gwaith Adnabod Lleferydd Uwch- IPA: [gaɬɨ], translation: further speech recognition work) project to develop speech recognition technology for the Welsh language. Wales has a population of around 3 million people, of whom around 20% speak Welsh (Office for National Statistics, 2012). Lesser-resourced languages typically lag in digital innovation, including in language technologies. However since 2012, the Welsh Government has updated and revised a strategy for supporting Welsh-language technology. Emphasis is placed on "more tools and resources … to facilitate the use of Welsh, including in the digital environment" (Welsh Government, 2012: 45) and "the development of new Welsh-language software applications and digital services" (Welsh Government, 2013; 12). With funding from the Welsh Government and S4C (the Welsh language television channel), the GALLU project aims to develop speech recognition technology for the Welsh language. The resources will be available under a permissive open-source licence, and will therefore be available for use in a broad spectrum of platforms and devices, including voice control for smart televisions.

2 Previous speech technology for Welsh

Prior to the GALLU project, the most substantial work on Welsh speech technology was developed under the WISPR (Welsh and Irish Speech Processing Resources) project (Prys et al., 2004). Previous work on a diphone-based synthesiser (Williams, 1994; 1995) and also a small speech database for Welsh (Williams, 1999) was built upon by the WISPR project. An improved synthetic Welsh voice was developed as part of the WISPR project as well as an MSAPI interface to Festival for use in Microsoft Windows environments (Bangor University Text to Speech, [no date]). Following the release of the WISPR resources under an open-source (BSD) licence, further work was facilitated to develop commercial Welsh voices by the Language Technologies Unit at Bangor University, by the Finnish company Bitlips (Bitlips Text to Speech, [no date]) and the Polish company Ivona (Ivona Text to Speech, [no date]). A "Basic Welsh speech recognition" (Bangor University, [no date]) project at the Language Technologies Unit at Bangor University in 2008-9 resulted in laboratory prototypes for a) a "command and control" application for a PC where applications could be launched by voice control and b) a simple voice-driven calculator. The GALLU project will build on this to develop further Welsh speech recognition resources.

Proceedings of the First Celtic Language Technology Workshop, pages 55–59,
Dublin, Ireland, August 23 2014.

3 Data design

The Welsh language has up to 29 consonants and a large number of vowels: up to 13 monophthongs and 13 diphthongs dependent on the variety (Awbery, 1984; Ball, 1984; Jones, 1984; Ball and Williams, 2001; Mayr and Davies, 2011; amongst others). In order to collect the appropriate data to train an acoustic model within HTK ([no date]), a set of phonetically rich words has been designed for contributors to read aloud. In designing the prompt set it was important to ensure that a small number of prompts contain representations of all of the phonemes in the language. The WISPR project's letter-to-sound rules were rewritten based on data mining from a lexicon, and a list of the most common sounds and words was extracted from a text corpus. The final prompt set will contain approximately 200 prompts (8 words per prompt) covering all of the phonemes in the language which may be recorded by contributors across different sessions.

{"identifier": "sample1", "text": u"lleuad, melyn, aelodau, siarad, ffordd, ymlaen, cefnogaeth, Helen"},
{"identifier": "sample2", "text": u"gwraig, oren, diwrnod, gwaith, mewn, eisteddfod, disgownt, iddo"},
{"identifier": "sample3", "text": u"oherwydd, Elliw, awdurdod, blynyddoedd, gwlad, tywysog, llyw, uwch"},
{"identifier": "sample4", "text": u"rhybuddio, Elen, uwchraddio, hwnnw, beic, Cymru, rhoi, aelod"},
{"identifier": "sample5", "text": u"rhai, steroid, cefnogaeth, felen, cau, garej, angau, ymhlith"},
{"identifier": "sample6", "text": u"gwneud, iawn, un, dweud, llais, wedi, gyda, llyn"},
{"identifier": "sample7", "text": u"lliw, yng Nghymru, gwneud, rownd, ychydig, wy, yn, llaes"},
{"identifier": "sample8", "text": u"hyn, newyddion, ar, roedd, pan, llun, melin, sychu"},
{"identifier": "sample9", "text": u"ychydig, glin, wrth, Huw, at, nhw, bod, bydd"}

Example 1: Display prompts within the Paldaruo application

A large pronunciation lexicon will be developed and used for speech recognition. The next steps for the project involve further data collection and linguistic model development.

4 Data collection: crowdsourcing and the Paldaruo Application

A large number of speakers are required in order to train the acoustic model which forms the basis of the speech recognition system. Recruiting speakers to attend a recording session at a sound booth with recording software can prove expensive and time consuming. In attempting to tackle this issue, a crowdsourcing approach is being used as a method for collecting data. Crowdsourcing is a low-cost and efficient way of collecting speech data.

A mobile application "Paldaruo" (Welsh for "chattering") has been developed for iOS and Android devices. Such devices, with inbuilt microphones and internet connectivity, provide a convenient mechanism for many volunteers to contribute speech corpus data. The app is optimised for ease of use in order to maximise potential contributions.

Each volunteer creates their own profile within the app providing metadata related to sex, age, linguistic characteristics and geographical background. Following this, the volunteers explicitly agree to their contributions being collected and used. The prompts, described above, are presented one at a time and the volunteer records each one individually. The recording is replayed and the volunteer verifies the quality or re-records. The user can stop and resume at any time. Prompts are provided to the volunteer in a random order; completed prompts will be included in the corpus even if the user does not record the full set.

The app accesses the microphone of the user's mobile device and records 48 kHz PCM files, which are sent to a server developed and hosted by the Language Technologies Unit at Bangor University. Uploads are queued in the background so that network speed issues do not interrupt the recording process.

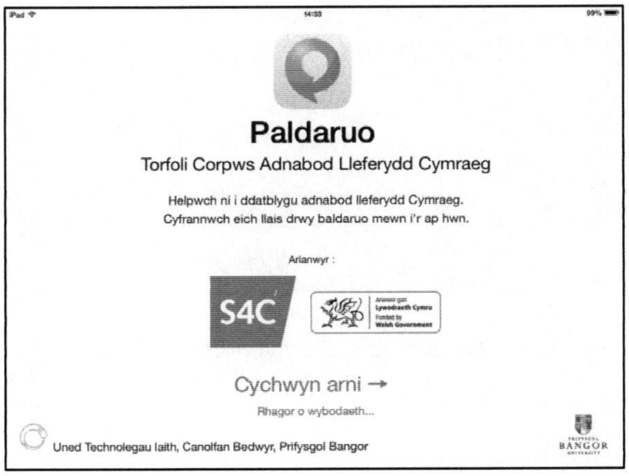

Translation:
Paldaruo
Crowdsourcing a Welsh speech recognition corpus

Help us to develop Welsh speech recognition.
Contribute your voice through nattering into this app.

Funders:
S4C Welsh Government

Begin >
More information...

Figure 1: Welcome screen in the Paldaruo App

The app was evaluated in a pilot application (see 5) and proved successful in obtaining a useful speech corpus from invited volunteers. However issues were highlighted with regards to background noise and recording volume levels. To address this, the app now includes background noise and volume level checks.

The official media launch of the app, with the final prompt set, will take place on 7th July 2014. There will be television coverage on S4C with high-profile individuals including the First Minister of Wales and celebrities providing endorsements and appeals for volunteers.

5 Data Application

5.1 Pilot Data Application

To date a small pilot speech corpus has been collected with the Paldaruo app covering the phonemes that appear in a vocabulary to control a robotic arm. 20 speakers contributed to this corpus and recorded 38 prompts (approx. 200 words) each, totalling around 4000 words. Certain commands, for instance 'up', exhibit dialect-dependent lexical variation, and in these cases every speaker recorded both regional forms.

Command:	Translation:
`golau ymlaen`	`light on`
`gafael agor`	`grip open`
`gafael cau`	`grip close`
`arddwrn i fyny / arddwrn lan`	`wrist up`
`arddwrn i lawr`	`wrist down`
`penelin i fyny / penelin lan`	`elbow up`
`penelin i lawr`	`elbow down`
`ysgwydd i fyny / ysgwydd lan`	`shoulder up`
`ysgwydd i lawr`	`shoulder down`
`troi i'r dde`	`turn to the right`
`troi i'r chwith`	`turn to the left`

This corpus has been used to develop a pilot speaker-independent Welsh-language speech recognition system for controlling the robotic arm. The pilot system uses HTK ([no date]) and Julius ([no date]), and follows the design of an existing English system (AonSquared, [no date]). It controls the robotic arm from a Raspberry Pi (a credit card-sized computer, popular in schools and coding clubs, costing around €35; see (Raspberry Pi Foundation, [No date]). The authors hope this simple demonstration will be recreated in schools and coding clubs for children throughout Wales, fitting in with the Welsh

Government's aim to support initiatives aimed at encouraging and supporting young people to engage "in the digital world in a Welsh-language context" (Welsh Government, 2013: 14).

5.2 Licensing

GALLU will follow the successful strategy of the WISPR project in using permissive open-source licensing. All outputs will be made available under the MIT licence (MIT, [No date]) which allows royalty-free use in both open-source and proprietary systems, including desktop computer software, web applications, mobile apps and embedded systems such as television set firmware.

This strategy allows the widest possible use of the project's outputs, and the maximal availability of Welsh speech recognition technology.

5.3 Application to other languages

The authors hope other lesser-resourced languages can harness the project's outputs and experience. The source code of the Paldaruo crowdsourcing app can easily be adapted for use in other languages. The process for developing the LVCSR system has been documented and will be published in the form of a tutorial. All project outputs, including the source code for the app, will be available under the MIT licence.

References

AonSquared. [No date]. *Speech recognition using the Raspberry Pi* [Online]. Available at: http://aonsquared.co.uk/raspi_voice_control [Accessed: 1 May 2014].

Bangor University [No date]. *Bangor University Basic Welsh Speech Recognition Project* [Online]. Available at: http://www.bangor.ac.uk/canolfanbedwyr/adllefsyl.php.en [Accessed: 1 May 2014].

Bangor University Text to Speech [No date] *Festival Demo voice* [Online]. Available at: http://www.e-gymraeg.org/siarad [Accessed: 1 May 2014].

Bitlips Text to Speeeh. [No date]. *Welsh Text to Speech Demo* [Online]. Available at: bitlips.fi/tts/demo-cy.cgi [Accessed: 1 May 2014].

Briony Williams. 1994. Diphone synthesis for the Welsh language. *Proceedings of the 1994 International Conference on Spoken Language Processing,* Yokohama, Japan: 739-742.

Briony Williams. 1995. Text-to-speech synthesis for Welsh and Welsh English. *Proceedings of Eurospeech 1995*, Madrid, Spain, 2: 1113-1116.

Briony Williams. 1999. A Welsh speech database: preliminary results. *Proceedings of Eurospeech 1999*, Budapest, Hungary, 5: 2283-2286.

Delyth Prys, Briony Williams, Bill Hicks, Dewi Jones, Ailbhe Ní Chasaide, Christer Gobl, Julie Carson-Berndsen, Fred Cummins, Máire Ní Chiosáin, John McKenna, Rónán Scaife and Elaine Uí Dhonnchadha. 2004. *SALTMIL Workshop at LREC 2004: First Steps in Language Documentation for Minority Languages.*

Glyn E. Jones. 1984. The distinctive vowels and consonants of Welsh. In Martin J. Ball and Glyn E. Jones (eds.). *Welsh phonology: Selected readings.* University of Wales Press, Cardiff, UK: 40-64.

Gwenllian M. Awbery. 1984. Phonotactic constraints in Welsh. In Martin J. Ball and Glyn E. Jones (eds.). *Welsh phonology: Selected readings.* University of Wales Press, Cardiff, UK. 65-104.

HTK. [No date]. *Hidden Markov Toolkit* [Online]. Available at: http://htk.eng.cam.ac.uk/ [Accessed: 1 May 2014].

Ivona Text to Speech. [No date]. *Text to Speech Portfolio* [Online]. Available at: http://www.ivona.com/en/ [Accessed: 1 May 2014].

Julius. [No date]. *Open-Source Large Vocabulary CSR Engine Julius* [Online]. Available at: http://julius.sourceforge.jp/en_index.php [Accessed: 1 May 2014].

Martin J. Ball and Briony Williams. 2001. *Welsh phonetics*. The Edwin Mellen Press, Lampeter, UK.

Martin J. Ball. 1984. Phonetics for phonology. In Martin J. Ball and Glyn E. Jones (eds.). *Welsh phonology: Selected readings*. University of Wales Press, Cardiff, UK.

MIT. [No date]. *The MIT License* [Online]. Available at: http://opensource.org/licenses/mit-license.html [Accessed: 1 May 2014].

Office for National Statistics. 2012. 2011 Census: Welsh language profile, unitary authorities in Wales. Available at: http://www.ons.gov.uk/ons/rel/census/2011-census/key-statistics-for-unitary-authorities-in-wales/rft-table-ks208wa.xls [Accessed: 1 May 2014].

Robert Mayr and Hannah Davies. 2011. A cross-dialectal acoustic study of the monophthongs and diphthongs of Welsh. *Journal of the International Phonetic Association,* 41(1): 1-25.

Raspberry Pi Foundation. [No date]. *What is a Raspberry Pi?* [Online]. Available at: http://www.raspberrypi.org/help/what-is-a-raspberry-pi/ [Accessed: 1 May 2014].

Welsh Government. 2012. *A living language, a language for living*. Available at: http://wales.gov.uk/docs/dcells/publications/122902wls201217en.pdf [Accessed: 1 May 2014].

Welsh Government. 2013. *Welsh language Technology and Digital Media Action Plan*. Available at: http://wales.gov.uk/docs/dcells/publications/230513-action-plan-en.pdf [Accessed: 20 June 2014].

gdbank: The beginnings of a corpus of dependency structures and type-logical grammar in Scottish Gaelic

Colin Batchelor
Royal Society of Chemistry, Cambridge, UK CB4 0WF
batchelorc@rsc.org

Abstract

We present gdbank, a small handbuilt corpus of 32 sentences with dependency structures and categorial grammar type assignments. The sentences have been chosen to illustrate as broad a range of the unusual features of Scottish Gaelic as possible, particularly nouns being used to represent psychological states where more thoroughly-studied languages such as English and French would prefer a verb, and prepositions marking aspect, as is also seen in Welsh and, for example, Irish Gaelic. We provide hand-built dependency trees, building on previous work on Irish Gaelic and using the Universal Dependency Scheme. We also provide a tentative categorial grammar account of the words in the sentences, based largely on previous work on English.

1 Introduction

Scottish Gaelic (usually hereafter Gaelic) is a Celtic language, rather closely related to Irish, with around 59,000 speakers as of the last UK census in 2011. As opposed to the situation for Irish Gaelic (Lynn et al., 2012a; Lynn et al., 2012b; Lynn et al., 2013; Lynn et al., 2014) there are no treebanks or tagging schemes for Scottish Gaelic, although there are machine-readable dictionaries and databases available from Sabhal Mòr Ostaig. A single paper in the ACL Anthology (Kessler, 1995) mentions Scottish Gaelic in the context of computational dialectology of Irish. There is also an LREC workshop paper (Scannell, 2006) on machine translation between Irish and Scottish Gaelic. Elsewhere in the Celtic languages, Welsh has an LFG grammar (Mittendorf and Sadler, 2005) but no treebanks. For Breton there is a small amount of work on morphological analysis and Constraint-Grammar-based machine translation (Tyers, 2010). Recent work on the grammar of Scottish Gaelic (for example (Adger and Ramchand, 2003; Adger and Ramchand, 2005), but there are many more examples) has largely focussed on theoretical syntactic issues somewhat distant from the more surfacy approaches popular in the field of natural language processing. This paper explores grammatical issues in Scottish Gaelic by means of dependency tagging and combinatory categorial grammar (CCG), which we see as complementary approaches. As such it is explicitly inspired by CCGbank (Hockenmaier and Steedman, 2007), which consists of dependency structures and CCG derivations for over 99% of the Penn Treebank. It is hoped that this corpus will be a useful adjunct to currently on-going work in developing a part-of-speech tagset and tagger for Scottish Gaelic.

Section 2 describes how the corpus was prepared, sections 3 and 4 give some context for the dependency scheme and categorial grammar annotations respectively, and the main part of the paper is section 5, which deals with language-specific features of the corpus.

2 Preparing the corpus

The corpus consists of a small handbuilt selection of sentences from the transcripts of *An Litir Bheag*, which is a weekly podcast from the BBC written by a native speaker and aimed at Gaelic learners, example sentences from (Lamb, 2003), the BBC's online news in Gaelic and the Gaelic column in the Scotsman newspaper. In order to illustrate as much of the interesting points of Scottish Gaelic as possible,

Proceedings of the First Celtic Language Technology Workshop, pages 60–65,
Dublin, Ireland, August 23 2014.

Dependency	Example	Gloss	GR
det	*gach latha* (det latha gach)	every day	det
dobj	*Ithidh i ìm* (dobj Ithidh ìm)	She eats butter	dobj
adpmod	*Tha piseag agam* (adpmod Tha agam)	I have a kitten	ncmod
adpobj	*às an eilean* (adpobj às eilean)	from the island	dobj
nsubj	*Tha mi a' dol* (Tha mi)	I am coming	ncsubj
prt	*Chan eil* (prt eil chan)	is not	ncmod
xcomp	*Tha mi ag iarraidh* (xcomp Tha iarraidh)	I want	xcomp
acomp	*Tha i breagha* (xcomp Tha breagha)	It is fine	xcomp
ccomp	*bheachd gun tigeadh e* (ccomp bheachd tigeadh)	thought he would come	ccomp
mark	*gun tigeadh e* (mark tigeadh gun)	that he would come	ncmod

Table 1: Examples of the UDS-based scheme in this paper mapped to the Briscoe and Carroll scheme.

we looked in particular for sentences describing psychological states and made sure that a reasonable number of the sentences used each verb for "to be", which we will illustrate in section 5.

The sentences are tokenized by hand using the following rules: (1) Punctuation which never forms part of a lexical item such as the comma, the full stop, the colon and the semicolon is always separated out from the previous word. (2) Strings connected by a hyphen, for example *h-Alba* in *Banca na h-Alba* (Bank of Scotland) or *t-Òban* as in *an t-Òban* (the town of Oban) are always kept together. (3) The apostrophe is kept together with the copula where it proceeds it, for example in *'S fhearr leam* (I like). (4) Because the past tense particle *do* is reduced to *dh'* before a vowel and before *f*, and this is always typographically closed up, we separate out past-tense *dh'* as its own token. These rules work for the small dataset described here but would clearly need to be expanded for work in the wild.

In this preliminary work the dependencies and types have been determined by a single, non-native speaker, annotator, according to a set of guidelines which were built up during the annotation process. This is clearly less than ideal, however, the guidelines are available along with the corpus and we hope to be able to get the input of a native speaker, not least for interannotator studies.

We use the CoNLL-X format (Buchholz and Marsi, 2006), leaving the POS and projective dependency fields empty and store the categorial grammar type under field 6, FEATS.

3 Dependency scheme

There are four dependency schemes that we consulted while preparing the corpus. The initial inspiration was provided by the C&C parser (Curran et al., 2007), which in addition to providing categorial grammar derivations for sentences provides a dependency structure in the GR (Grammatical Representation) scheme due to (Briscoe and Carroll, 2000; Briscoe and Carroll, 2002). This contains 23 types and was developed originally for parser evaluation. Another popular scheme is the Stanford Dependency scheme (de Marneffe and Manning, 2008; de Marneffe and Manning, 2013), which is more finely-grained with over twice the number of dependency types to deal specifically with noisy data and to make it more accessible to non-linguists building information extraction applications. A very important scheme is the Dublin scheme for Irish (Lynn et al., 2012a; Lynn et al., 2012b; Lynn et al., 2013), which is of a similar size to the Stanford scheme, but the reason for its size relative to GR is that it includes a large number of dependencies intended to handle grammatical features found in Irish but not in English. Lastly we mention the Universal Dependency Scheme developed in (McDonald et al., 2013), which we have adopted, despite its being coarser-grained than the Dublin scheme, on account of its simplicity and utility for cross-lingual comparisons and cross-training (Lynn et al., 2014).

Table 1 gives examples of the dependency relations used along with their mapping to the GR scheme.

4 Categorial grammar

Combinatory categorial grammar (CCG) is a type-logical system which was developed to represent natural languages such as English but has subsequently been extended to other systems such as chord sequences in jazz (Granroth-Wilding and Steedman, 2012). For a full description the reader is referred to (Steedman and Baldridge, 2003), but in order to follow the rest of this paper you merely need to know that the type `N/N` is a function which takes an argument of `N` to its right, returning `N`, and that the type `N\N` is a function expecting an argument of `N` to its left and that these are combined by application, composition, where `A/B` combines with `B/C` to yield `A/C`, and type-raising where `N` is converted to `T/(N\T)`. Attractive features of CCG for modelling a less-well-studied language include that it is a lexical theory in which it is the lexicon contains the rules for how words are combined to make sense rather than an external grammar, that it allows all manner of unconventional constituents, which is particularly powerful for parsing coordinated structures in English, that it is equivalent to a weakly context-sensitive grammar and hence has the power of a real natural language. In Steedman and Baldridge (2003) there are examples of the application of multimodal CCG to Irish Gaelic. However, to the best of our knowledge this paper is the first application of CCG to Scottish Gaelic.

In gdbank, there is a single hand-built CCG derivation for every sentence. The notation is based on that in CCGbank with a small number of adaptations for Gaelic (see next section). The basic units that can be assembled into types are `S` (clauses), `N` (nouns), `conj` (conjugations), and `PP` (prepositional phrases). For subcategorization purposes and to help keep things clear for the annotator and the reader we mark prepositional phrases with the dictionary form of the preposition.

We have not yet investigated overgeneration and ungrammatical sentences, hence there is only one kind of modality in gdbank; however restricting the way words can combine to the way in which they actually do combine in Gaelic is an obvious and essential next step.

5 Language-specific features

Prepositional phrases in Gaelic are often single-word, fused preposition–pronouns, a part-of-speech found across the Celtic languages. An ambiguous case of this is the token *ris*, which can be either *ri* with the pronoun *e*, hence taking the CCG type PP[ri], or the pre-determiner form of *ri*, hence PP[ri]/N[b]. The other class of fused preposition–pronoun we need to consider is that in sentences like *Tha mi gad chluinntinn*, "I can hear you", where *gad* is *ag* fused with *do* "your". In this case it has type PP[ag]/S[n]. Adjectives as in CCGbank are treated as clauses, `S[adj]`. The verbal noun is labelled `S[n]` by analogy with Hockenmaier and Steedman (2007). In addition to declarative and interrogative clauses, `S[dcl]` and `S[q]`, we take our lead from the fourfold division of preverbal particles and add negative clauses `S[neg]`, usually introduced by *cha* or *chan*, and negative interrogative clauses, `S[negq]`, introduced by *nach*.

There are two verbs for "to be" in Scottish Gaelic, *bi* and *is*. *Bi* is used for predicate statements about nouns, to forming the present tense and to describe some psychological states. It does not usually equate two NPs, with an exception we will come to. In the Dublin scheme the prepositional phrase headed by *ag* in *Tá sé ag iascaireacht* ("He is fishing.") is treated as being an externally-controlled complement of *Tá* (Gaelic *tha*) and we carry this analysis over into Scottish Gaelic where this is the most common way of expressing the present tense. Figure 1 demonstrates this, where *dhachaigh* is a non-clausal modifier of *dol*, the verbal noun for "to go". *Is* can be used as the copula between two NPs, and to express psychological states such as liking and preference. To say "I am a teacher", the Gaelic is *'S e tidsear a th' annam.* This, at least on the surface, equates pronoun *e*, with a noun described by a relative clause including the verb *bi*. Fig. 1 shows our dependency tree for this. Note that this is different from the scheme in Lynn et al. (2012b) because of a difference between the two languages. They treat the analogous sentence *Is tusa an múinteoir* "You are the teacher" as having a subject, "the teacher", and a clausal predicate, *tusa*, "you indeed".

The most straightforward way of expressing a preference is the assertive *is* followed by an adjective or noun, a PP marking the preferrer, and then the object. If you dislike music, you might say *Is beag orm ceòl.* There are exactly analogous constructions in Irish with *is* + adjective + PP[le] + object, for example *Is maith liom...* "I like...", which in (Uí Dhonnchadha, 2009) is treated as having the prepositional phrase as the subject and the adjective as predicate. We modify this to use `adpmod` as in the Universal Dependency Scheme as shown in Fig. 1.

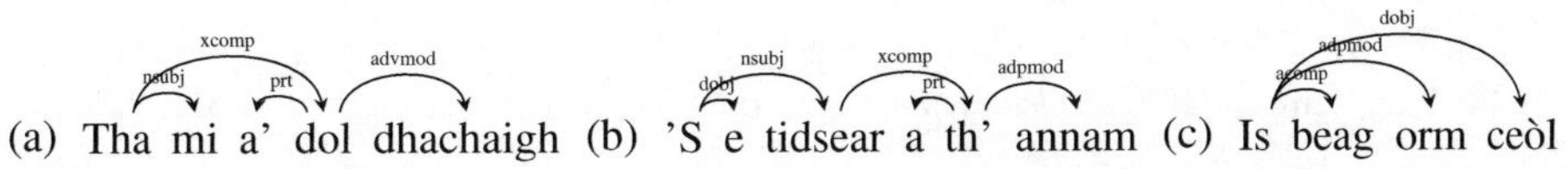

Figure 1: Dependency trees for (a) "I am going home", (b) "I am a teacher" and (c) "I hate music".

Type	Count	Notes	Type	Count	Notes
`N`	104	noun	`N\N`	13	adjective/genitive noun
`PP/N`	41	preposition	`PP/S[n]`	10	*ag/a'/air* etc.
`N/N`	38	determiner	`S[dep]/PP/N`	8	*bi, is* (after particle)
.	31	.	`(N\N)/S[dcl]`	7	relative
`S[dcl]/PP/N`	25	*bi, is*	`S[n]`	7	intransitive verbal noun
`PP`	18	PP	`(N\N)/(N\N)`	7	genitive article

Table 2: Counts for most common types found in corpus. `PP[air]`, `PP[aig]` and so on have been merged.

6 Conclusions and future work

In this paper we have presented a small handbuilt corpus of Scottish Gaelic sentences, their dependency structures and their CCG derivations. To the best of our knowledge this represents the first attempt to handle a range of real-life Scottish Gaelic sentences in such a way. gdbank itself and the guidelines used to build it are available from `https://code.google.com/p/gdbank/` and we welcome feedback. We have of course only been able to illustrate a small number of constructions. Tables 2 and 3 list counts for the categorial types and dependency relations used. In 32 sentences there are a total of 406 tokens.

We have not yet on the other hand attempted to deal with the morphology of Scottish Gaelic, for example lenition and slenderization, beyond drawing the attention of the human annotator to these phenomena when they may affect the correct parsing of a sentence. Clearly for automated natural-language processing of Gaelic these will need to be treated programmatically. We also disregard case and gender, although we expect that these will be dealt with as part of a rather more ambitious project, that of the Lamb group at the University of Edinburgh to build a part-of-speech tagset and tagged corpus which we look forward to seeing.

Acknowledgements

The anonymous referees for their very constructive comments.

Relation	Count	Relation	Count	Relation	Count
adpmod	58	mark	23	amod	11
nsubj	47	nmod	18	advmod	9
adpobj	38	ccomp	17	acomp	7
det	34	prt	14	cc	6
p	33	dobj	13	rcmod	4
ROOT	32	xcomp	13	appos	2

Table 3: Counts for dependency relations in gdbank. Note the high number of `adpmod` relations which is significantly larger than `adpobj` because of fused preposition–pronouns in Gaelic.

References

David Adger and Gillian Ramchand. 2003. Predication and equation. *Linguistic Enquiry*, 34:325–359.

David Adger and Gillian Ramchand. 2005. Psych nouns and predications. In *Proceedings of the 36th Annual Meeting of the North East Linguistic Society*, Amherst, MA, October.

Ted Briscoe and John Carroll. 2000. Grammatical relation annotation. Online at http://www.sussex.ac.uk/Users/johnca/grdescription/index.html.

Ted Briscoe and John Carroll. 2002. Robust accurate statistical annotation of general text. In *Proceedings of the Third International Conference on Language Resources and Evaluation (LREC'02)*, Las Palmas, Canary Islands, Spain, May.

Sabine Buchholz and Erwin Marsi. 2006. CoNLL-X shared task on multilingual dependency parsing. In *Proceedings of the Tenth Conference on Computational Natural Language Learning*, New York, NY, June.

James Curran, Stephen Clark, and Johan Bos. 2007. Linguistically motivated large-scale NLP with C&C and Boxer. In *Proceedings of the 45th Annual Meeting of the Association for Computational Linguistics Companion Volume Proceedings of the Demo and Poster Sessions*, pages 33–36, Prague, Czech Republic, June. Association for Computational Linguistics.

Marie-Catherine de Marneffe and Christopher D. Manning. 2008. The Stanford typed dependencies representation. In *Coling 2008: Proceedings of the workshop on Cross-Framework and Cross-Domain Parser Evaluation*, pages 1–8, Manchester, UK, August. Coling 2008 Organizing Committee.

Marie-Catherine de Marneffe and Christopher D. Manning. 2013. Stanford typed dependencies manual. Online at http://nlp.stanford.edu/software/dependencies_manual.pdf.

Mark Granroth-Wilding and Mark Steedman. 2012. Statistical parsing for harmonic analysis of jazz chord sequences. In *Proceedings of the International Computer Music Conference*, pages 478–485. International Computer Music Association, September.

Julia Hockenmaier and Mark Steedman. 2007. CCGBank: A corpus of CCG derivations and dependency structures extracted from the Penn Treebank. *Computational Linguistics*, 33:355–356.

Brett Kessler. 1995. Computational dialectology in Irish Gaelic. In *Seventh Conference of the European Chapter of the Association for Computational Linguistics*, page 60, Dublin, Ireland, March.

William Lamb. 2003. *Scottish Gaelic, 2nd edn*. Lincom Europa, Munich, Germany.

Teresa Lynn, Ozlem Cetinoglu, Jennifer Foster, Elaine Uí Dhonnchadha, Mark Dras, and Josef van Genabith. 2012a. Irish treebanking and parsing: A preliminary evaluation. In Nicoletta Calzolari, Khalid Choukri, Thierry Declerck, Mehmet Uğur Doğan, Bente Maegaard, Joseph Mariani, Jan Odijk, and Stelios Piperidis, editors, *Proceedings of the Eighth International Conference on Language Resources and Evaluation (LREC-2012)*, pages 1939–1946, Istanbul, Turkey, May. European Language Resources Association (ELRA). ACL Anthology Identifier: L12-1189.

Teresa Lynn, Jennifer Foster, Mark Dras, and Elaine Uí Dhonnchadha. 2012b. Active learning and the irish treebank. In *Proceedings of the Australasian Language Technology Association Workshop 2012*, pages 23–32, Dunedin, New Zealand, December.

Teresa Lynn, Jennifer Foster, and Mark Dras. 2013. Working with a small dataset - semi-supervised dependency parsing for Irish. In *Proceedings of the Fourth Workshop on Statistical Parsing of Morphologically-Rich Languages*, pages 1–11, Seattle, Washington, USA, October. Association for Computational Linguistics.

Teresa Lynn, Jennifer Foster, Mark Dras, and Lamia Tounsi. 2014. Cross-lingual transfer parsing for low-resourced languages: An Irish case study. In *Proceedings of Celtic Language Technology Workshop 2014*, Dublin, Ireland, August.

Ryan McDonald, Joakim Nivre, Yvonne Quirmbach-Brundage, Yoav Goldberg, Dipanjan Das, Kuzman Ganchev, Keith Hall, Slav Petrov, Hao Zhang, Oscar Täckström, Claudia Bedini, Núria Bertomeu Castelló, and Jungmee Lee. 2013. Universal dependency annotation for multilingual parsing. In *Proceedings of the 51st Annual Meeting of the Association for Computational Linguistics (Volume 2: Short Papers)*, pages 92–97, Sofia, Bulgaria, August. Association for Computational Linguistics.

Ingo Mittendorf and Louisa Sadler. 2005. The Welsh PARGRAM grammar. In *12th Welsh Syntax Workshop*, Gregynog, Wales, July.

Kevin P. Scannell. 2006. Machine translation for closely related language pairs. In *Proceedings of the LREC 2006 Workshop on Strategies for developing machine translation for minority languages*, pages 103–107, Genoa, Italy, May.

Mark Steedman and Jason Baldridge. 2003. Combinatory Categorial Grammar. Online at http://homepages.inf.ed.ac.uk/steedman/papers/ccg/SteedmanBaldridgeNTSyntax.pdf.

F. M. Tyers. 2010. Rule-based Breton to French machine translation. In *Proceeedings of the 14th Annual Conference of the European Association of Machine Translation, EAMT10*, pages 174–181, Saint-Raphaël, France, May.

Elaine Uí Dhonnchadha. 2009. *Part-of-speech tagging and partial parsing for Irish using finite-state transducers and constraint grammar*. Ph.D. thesis, Dublin City University.

Developing high-end reusable tools and resources for Irish-language terminology, lexicography, onomastics (toponymy), folkloristics, and more, using modern web and database technologies

Brian Ó Raghallaigh
Dublin City University
brian.oraghallaigh@dcu.ie

Michal Boleslav Měchura
Dublin City University
michal.boleslav.mechura@dcu.ie

Abstract

Irish, a low-resourced lesser-used language, is striving to punch above its weight when it comes to some of the digital language tools and resources available to its users. High-tech language tools and resources for Irish are being developed in a number of universities in Ireland and elsewhere, in language technology areas relating to search, parsing, proofing, speech, translation, etc. (Judge at al., 2012). This paper aims to highlight work done by researchers at Fiontar, Dublin City University (DCU), to make a number of valuable Irish-language terminological, lexicographical, onomastic, and folkloristic data stocks more readily accessible, usable, and manageable using web and database technologies. Tools built with these technologies have facilitated the re-organisation, distributed development, and more widespread dissemination of these data stocks, as well as the creation of new data stocks. These language tools, which are on a par with tools that are available to users of well-resourced languages (take for example the online interface of the multilingual terminology database of the European Union, *IATE*: http://iate.europa.eu/), are now enabling Irish language users, language professionals, and linguists operate in an environment similar to that of their major language counterparts. The public interfaces of all Irish-language tools and resources developed by Fiontar are made available at http://www.gaois.ie/.

1 Introduction

Although Irish is a low-resourced language, the Irish Government's *20 Year Strategy for the Irish Language*, which prioritises the "promotion and protection" of the language (Government of Ireland, 2010), has brought about investment in the creation of digital language tools and resources. Linguistic resources, such as printed dictionaries, are now being made available electronically through retro-digitisation, or being created digitally, and then enhanced with search engines powered by language technologies, such as spelling error detection.

This paper highlights the work done by researchers at Fiontar, Dublin City University (DCU) in the identification of valuable non-digital language resources, the digitisation of these resources where necessary, and the application of web, database, and language technology to these resources to widen access and availability, and to increase effectiveness and usability.

Fiontar's tools and resources include public websites that provide easy, user-friendly access to Irish-language terminological, lexicographical, onomastic, and folkloristic data stocks, as well as web-based tools for managing and developing this data. User-friendliness is seen by Fiontar as key in the promotion of the language on the Internet (Měchura and Ó Raghallaigh, 2009). Single query, all-in-one Google-like search, is also a priority, with sophisticated quick search being a feature on all Fiontar websites. All of Fiontar's digital language tools and resources are made available at or linked to from http://www.gaois.ie/ (*gaois* 'wisdom').

2 Terminology and lexicography

In 2005, in partnership with Foras na Gaeilge, the body responsible for the promotion of the Irish lan-

Proceedings of the First Celtic Language Technology Workshop, pages 66–70,
Dublin, Ireland, August 23 2014.

guage throughout the whole island of Ireland, researchers at Fiontar began development of the National Terminology Database for Irish, *focal.ie* (*focal* 'word'). Retro-digitisation (where a work that was previously published on paper is converted into a digital, computer-readable format) was carried out on 54 different dictionaries and term lists supplied by the Terminology Committee of Foras na Gaeilge (Bhreathnach, 2007), and the dataset was imported into a purpose-built relational database for terminological and lexicographical data (Měchura, 2006). In addition, two web-based interfaces to the new database were developed. The first, a password-protected web application, provided a geographically dispersed group of authorised terminologists with access to the data as well as a set of web-based tools for editing and developing the data. The second, a public website, gave public access to the data via a set of linguistically sophisticated (e.g. inflection awareness, misspelling detection, language selection) search tools (Měchura, 2008; Měchura and Ó Raghallaigh, 2010). This meant that for the first time, Irish-language users, most notably language professionals, had free and searchable worldwide electronic access to this valuable data stock.

The focal.ie system continues to be maintained and developed today. The database currently contains over 342,000 terms, mostly in Irish and English. The technology has gone through a number of major overhauls. Most notably, the database and (private) editorial interface were replaced in 2012 with a new system called *Léacslann* (Měchura, 2012b). In Léacslann, terminological data is now stored as XML. Léacslann also incorporates additional features such as user permission management, a power search feature which allows users to interrogate the data in complex ways, and an extranet application to gather input from external subject and language experts. And in 2013, the public search algorithm was optimised for speed and enhanced with better spelling-error detection.

One of the advantages of the Léacslann system is that multiple data stocks can be stored and managed in the same database. This allows the editorial tools to be reused across multiple terminology and lexicography projects. The system now hosts multiple lexical databases being maintained and developed by Fiontar language experts. It also has the potential to be used to host terminology and lexicography projects for other institutions and languages, as it is flexible and customisable. It can be used to work with various kinds of stocks such as monolingual and bilingual dictionaries, terminology databases or indeed any sort of reference work. Léacslann stocks can accommodate any language and any combination of languages, as long as text in those languages can be encoded in Unicode (Měchura, 2012b). This might prove to be an economical way to develop such resources for other low-resourced languages such as Scottish Gaelic, for example.

Corpora for use in lexicography have also been developed. One such corpus, a parallel Irish-English corpus of Irish and European legal texts, made available to Fiontar by the Irish Government and the European Commission, known as *ParaDocs*, has been made available to the public on gaois.ie.

3 Onomastics

In 2007, in partnership with the Placenames Branch of the Government of Ireland, the body that conducts research into the placenames of Ireland to provide authoritative Irish language versions of those placenames for official and public use, researchers at Fiontar began development of the Placenames Database of Ireland, *logainm.ie* (*logainm* 'placename'). A new relational database for bilingual Irish-English toponymic data was purpose-built for the project, and data already digitised by the Placenames Branch was imported into this database (Mac Giolla Easpaig, 2009). The architecture adopted for the terminology project was reflected in the placenames project in that two web interfaces, one public and one private (editorial), were built on top of the placenames database to allow dissemination as well as distributed editing and development of the data via the web (Měchura and Ó Raghallaigh, 2012).

A mapping interface, which used Google maps, was added to the public website in 2010, and in 2014, the data structure was enhanced with the inclusion of *place clusters*. These so-called clusters better reflect how people think about 'places' such as *Donegal*, for example. People don't normally think about the distinction between the various administrative units called 'Donegal' in County Donegal (i.e. the parish, townland, town, and electoral division), all of which are stored as distinct objects in the placenames database, but rather think of just one place, Donegal. The new data structure allows clustered place objects to be grouped and presented in a more user-friendly way (Měchura, 2012a).

Other developments include a collaboration with the Digital Repository of Ireland to make the dataset available as Linked Data, i.e. as exposed RDF data objects that are linked to equivalent objects in other geodatasets such as GeoNames (Lopes et al., 2013), and a project to match the dataset with Ordnance Survey Ireland so that logainm.ie data can be displayed on OSi maps, and in turn so that those maps can be used in place of Google Maps on the website (Byrne et al., 2013). As of May 2014, the English and Irish versions of the OSi medium-scale *Basemap* are being used on logainm.ie in place of Google Maps (Satellite View).

Data, some of which has to be digitised (originating on maps or on hand-written cards, for example), continues to be added to the placenames database, and development is ongoing. Additional resources such as maps, articles, and educational resources are also added periodically. The database currently contains entries for over 108,000 geographic places on the island of Ireland.

Another onomastic project, which has recently been established aims to produce a surnames database, which will group related Irish and English surnames. The intention is to use the database to enhance the names search interface to the folklore collection described in Section 4, and to make this database freely available to search or to download and reuse. The project is in its infancy and will be fully reported on at a later date.

4 Folkloristics

In 2012, in partnership with the the National Folklore Collection (NFC) at University College Dublin, home to one of the largest collections of oral and ethnological material in the world, researchers at Fiontar began development of *dúchas.ie* (*dúchas* 'heritage'), a new digital version of the NFC. The project was initially funded by the Government Department of Arts, Heritage and the Gaeltacht on a pilot basis for one year (2012-13) and has now been funded from the same source for three more years (2013-16) to digitise, digitally catalogue, and publish online 14% of the NFC. The NFC comprises multiple collections, including a music archive, a map archive, an audio and video archive, a collection of paintings, and a collection of photographs. One collection in particular, a manuscript collection comprising handwritten stories, gathered as part of a Government-sponsored scheme in 1937-39, has been chosen as the first collection to be migrated to dúchas.ie. Known as *The Schools' Collection*, it was chosen primarily due to its popularity (Ó Cléircín et al., forthcoming).

Since The Schools' Collection comprises manuscript only, digitisation in its case involves the scanning of pages to create digital image files. The text written on these pages is not being transcribed, as this would be not be feasible, but a digital catalogue of the pages and the stories written on them is being compiled as part of the project, to make the collection electronically searchable. It is envisaged that 46% of the Schools' Collection, i.e. *c.* 339,000 pages, will be scanned and catalogued by 2016.

As with the terminology/lexicography and the placenames projects, the dúchas.ie project comprises two web applications, one public and one private (editorial), and two databases, one for each web application. The public system is used to present the digitised collections to the world, and provides the user with a number of search interfaces. Currently, The Schools' Collection can be searched by *person* (the names of the people who told or collected the stories) or by *place* (where the stories were collected). The private system is used to manage and edit the digital catalogue. The contents of the private database are transferred to the public database weekly. In this instance, the Léacslann platform was reused, and a customised editorial/management application was added for this data stock.

5 Digitisation, management, and dissemination

Expertise in digitisation project management, as well as web-based data management and publication has allowed Fiontar to transition other Irish language legacy data stocks to the web. One example is the biographies database, *ainm.ie* (*ainm* 'name'). This project involved the digitisation of nine physical volumes of biographies (*c.* 1,700 lives) written and published between 1986 and 2007. Once again, this resource has been digitised, managed online, and published online with associated electronic browsing, navigation, and search tools, all of which involved the reuse of existing infrastructure, technologies, and expertise. Another example is the legacy research sound archive of the Placenames Branch, which is accessible to researchers at http://www.logainm.ie/phono/.

6 Technologies and hosting

All of the projects described here were built using web and database technologies. The Microsoft .NET Framework and SQL Server platform were used in each case. Hosting for all websites and databases is provided by DCU Information Systems and Services in conjunction with the HEAnet. Binary files created for the dúchas.ie project are hosted by UCD Research IT.

7 Conclusion

This paper described some of the tools and resources for Irish developed and made available online by Fiontar, Dublin City University, as well as the web and database technologies utilised in their deployment. It was highlighted that all of these tools and resources encompass technologically and linguistically sophisticated search interfaces. The use of technology in this way to enhance the resources available to Irish-language users and professionals is serving to place their language-related activities on a more level playing field with their major language counterparts, and goes some way towards the promotion and protection of the language.

Acknowledgements

This research was undertaken with support from Fiontar, Dublin City University. The research described here is being undertaken with financial support from Foras na Gaeilge and from the Department of Arts, Heritage and the Gaeltacht of the Government of Ireland.

References

Úna Bhreathnach. 2007. www.focal.ie – A New Resource for Irish. *Translation Ireland*, 17(2):11-18.

Maria Byrne, Brian Ó Raghallaigh and Mairéad Nic Lochlainn. 2012. Synchronising the Ordnance Survey Ireland (OSi) and Placenames Branch (logainm.ie) bilingual toponymic datasets. In *Placenames Workshop: Management and dissemination of toponymic data online*. Dublin: 153-162.

Government of Ireland. 2010. *20-Year Strategy for the Irish Language 2010-2030*. Online at http://www.ahg.gov.ie/en/20-YearStrategyfortheIrishLanguage2010-2030/ [Retrieved 9 May 2014]

John Judge, Ailbhe Ní Chasaide, Rose Ní Dhubhda, Kevin P. Scannell and Elaine Uí Dhonnchadha. 2012. *The Irish Language in the Digital Age*. Springer, London, UK.

Nuno Lopes, Rebecca Grant, Brian Ó Raghallaigh, Eoghan Ó Carragáin, Sandra Collins and Stefan Decker. 2013. Linked Logainm: Enhancing Library Metadata using Linked Data of Irish Place Names. In *Linking and Contextualizing Publications and Datasets (LCPD 2013)*. September 2013, Malta.

Dónall Mac Giolla Easpaig. 2009. Ireland's heritage of geographical names. *Geographical Names as a Part of the Cultural Heritage, Wiener Schriften zur Geographie und Kartographie*, 18:79-85.

Michal Boleslav Měchura. 2006. Finding the right structure for lexicographical data: experiences from a terminology project. In *Proceedings of the 12th Euralex International Congress*. Torino: 189-198.

Michal Boleslav Měchura. 2008. Giving Them What They Want: Search Strategies for Electronic Dictionaries. In *Proceedings of the 13th Euralex International Congress*. Barcelona: 1295-1299.

Michal Boleslav Měchura and Brian Ó Raghallaigh. 2009. User-Friendliness: the key to promoting a minority language on the Internet. In *International Conference on Minority Languages (ICML 12)*. May 2009, Tartu.

Michal Boleslav Měchura and Brian Ó Raghallaigh. 2010. The Focal.ie National Terminology Database for Irish: software demonstration. In *Proceedings of the 14th Euralex International Congress*. Leewarden: 937-948.

Michal Boleslav Měchura and Brian Ó Raghallaigh. 2012. The logainm.ie Placenames Database of Ireland: software demonstration. In *Placenames Workshop: Management and dissemination of toponymic data online*. Dublin: 115-122.

Michal Boleslav Měchura. 2012a. Landscapes, languages and data structures: Issues in building the Placenames Database of Ireland. In *Digital Humanities Conference (DH 2012)*. July 2012, Hamburg.

Michal Boleslav Měchura. 2012b. Léacslann: a platform for building dictionary writing systems. In *Proceedings of the 15th Euralex International Congress*. Oslo: 855-861.

Gearóid Ó Cléircín, Anna Bale and Brian Ó Raghallaigh. Forthcoming. Dúchas.ie: ré nua i stair Chnuasach Bhéaloideas Éireann. *Béaloideas*.

DECHE and the Welsh National Corpus Portal

Delyth Prys
Language Technologies Unit
Canolfan Bedwyr
Bangor University
Wales
d.prys@bangor.ac.uk

Mared Roberts
Language Technologies Unit
Canolfan Bedwyr
Bangor University
Wales
mared.roberts@bangor.ac.uk

Dewi Bryn Jones
Language Technologies Unit
Canolfan Bedwyr
Bangor University
Wales
d.b.jones@bangor.ac.uk

Abstract

This paper describes the on-going project on Digitization, E-publishing and Electronic Corpus (DECHE). It also describes the building of a common infrastructure and portal for displaying and disseminating other Welsh language and bilingual Welsh/English text corpora. An overview is given of other corpora included in the on-line corpus portal, as well as corpora intended for future publication through the portal site. This is done within the context of developing resources frugally and efficiently for less-resourced languages.

1 Introduction

Electronic language corpora are some of the most essential resources both for contemporary linguistic research and the development of new language technology applications. They also present a challenge to Welsh and other Celtic languages as smaller languages that are invariably under-resourced with regards to the availability of and interest in funding language technologies. Existing resources need to be recycled, updated, and presented in accessible formats in order to be useful to a new generation of researchers. Although the whole world wide web is now, in some sense, available as an on-line corpus (Gatto, 2014), and that notable attempts have been made to use it to build linguistic corpora, foremost amongst them Kevin Scannell's Crúbadán Project for less resourced languages (Scannell, 2007), we believe that there is still a need for specific text corpora in different domains and for various uses that are easily searchable and accessible to a wide academic community and beyond. This paper provides a brief overview of how a piecemeal collection of Welsh corpora are being brought together into a coherent, online, freely accessible and expanding Welsh National Corpus Portal (Porth Corpora Cenedlaethol Cymru, [no date])

2. From the first corpus to National Portal

The catalyst for the development of the Welsh National Corpus Portal was the awarding of a grant for the DECHE Project. DECHE (Digido, E-gyhoeddi a Chorpws Electronig, translated as Digitization, E-publishing and Electronic Corpus), is funded by Y Coleg Cymraeg Cenedlaethol (The Welsh National College). This is a virtual college established by the Welsh Government in 2011 to promote and deliver Welsh-medium university education in Wales, including the creation of new Welsh language academic resources. The primary aim of the DECHE project is to produce e-books out of Welsh language scholarly, academic books which are out of print and unlikely to be reprinted in traditional paper format. Candidates for producing as e-books are nominated by lecturers working though the medium of Welsh, and prioritized by the Coleg Cymraeg, according to best fit with the Coleg's Academic Development Plan (Coleg Cymraeg Cenedlaethol, 2011). The current project processes around 30 books a year, which are published on Y Porth (Y Porth, [no date]), the Coleg's own portal website for Welsh academic teaching resources. Books are scanned at the National Library of Wales, and passed to the project's purpose built OCR software. Human based proofreading and corrections are made before final publishing into E-PUB (readable by most e-readers) and Mobi (for Kindle) formats. PDFs are also produced for the purpose of printing personal copies.

2.1 DECHE Corpus of Welsh Scholarly Writing

The creation of a corpus of academic Welsh writing (named DECHE Corpus of Welsh Scholarly Writing) is a spin off from this primary e-book activity, taking advantage of the fact that these books are being digitized in any case for another purpose. The original OCR process produces a text which still contains many errors, especially in dealing with Welsh accented characters and other linguistic peculiarities. Therefore the human proofreading stage is vital in producing high quality and clean text. Human involvement in the workflow allows in addition for metadata such as the book title, author, date of publication, keywords, and subject fields, as well as limited annotations within the text body to be input into the corpus. To date 30 books have been added into the corpus, giving a total of approximately 450,000 words. This total will rise annually during the lifetime of the project.

2.2 Welsh National Corpus Portal

The Welsh National Corpus Portal was developed as a means of fulfilling not only the secondary objectives of the DECHE project, but also to serve for the first time as an opportunity to plan and present other Welsh language related corpus resources. The corpus portal was inspired by the Welsh National Terminology Portal (Porth Termau Cenedlaethol Cymru, [no date]), which serves as an online one stop shop for displaying and searching tens of standardized terminology dictionaries. Although websites such as that of SketchEngine (Kilgarriff et al, 2004) provide an overarching interface to query many corpora in a number of languages, including Welsh, they deal mainly with major languages with ample corpus resources. Many smaller languages are still poorly endowed with corpus resources of any kind, and the Welsh National Corpus Portal seems a rare example of an attempt to bring together disparate resources for such a language.

The Welsh National Corpus Portal infrastructure supports importing text resources as well as a search tool for both monolingual and bilingual corpora. A corpus management interface was developed in-house in order to facilitate tasks such as importing texts to the on-line corpora, using a 'submit to website' button by project staff, without the intervention of software experts. In the case of the DECHE corpus, the infrastructure supports importing the finally published e-pub files. Publication level metadata is also collected and stored in the infrastructure with imported texts. In the case of bilingual corpora, CSV and TMX file formats are supported.

The corpus portal's search and import functionalities employ natural language processing components for segmentation and lemmatization. The segmentation tool was originally developed in-house for use in translation memory software, and the lemmatizer was originally developed for the Cysill grammar and spelling program. Lemmatization enables searching through the Portal's Welsh language texts for all forms of a given search word, including mutations forms and conjugated verbs. For example, typing in 'canu' (to sing) will also return all possible forms of the lemma, including 'cenir' (present impersonal form of the verb), 'ganodd' third person past tense with soft mutation, 'nghanu' (verb noun form with a nasal mutation) and 'cheni' (second person present form of the verb with a spirant mutation).

3 Other published corpora

3.1 Criteria for including corpora in the National Portal

To date, only corpora developed at the LTU itself, or that the LTU has inherited responsibility for, are included in the Portal. This is for practical reasons, in that these corpora have been designed or adapted in house specifically for inclusion in the Portal, their format is compatible with that of the Portal.

Other useful Welsh corpora available on-line are listed on the web-site, with a link provided to their own web-sites. It is hoped in future that corpora from other sources will become available for inclusion in the National Portal, and that information about other unpublished corpora will also be made available there.

3.2 The CEG corpus

The first major Welsh electronic corpus to be collected was the CEG (Corpws Electroneg o'r Gymraeg) corpus in the early 1990s (Ellis, N.C. et al. 2001). This was designed as a lexical and word count corpus of samples of around 2,000 word segments from various genres of fiction and non-fiction resulting in a 1 million word corpus. This was innovative in its time and together with an associated part of speech tagger and lemmatizer, was a major contribution to Welsh corpus studies. However, as time went by CEG became difficult to access and use, and due to numerous requests for help from individual scholars, the decision was made to port it, together with the attendant metadata, into the Welsh National Corpus Portal. The original CEG files and data however were also ported to a new server and have been maintained on-line in addition to the new format.

3.3 The National Assembly for Wales Record parallel text corpora

Similar to the Hansard produced by the UK parliament at Westminster, the National Assembly of Wales produce and publish a bilingual record of its main chamber's proceedings. Assembly members may speak in either Welsh or English. Their words are transcribed and translated into the other language, creating a bilingual record of what is said. The written proceedings are carefully translated and edited, and thus provide an excellent resource for a variety of research and development purposes.

An early version of a parallel text corpus from the National Assembly of Wales Record was created by Jones and Eisele in 2006 (Jones et al, 2006). This covered the period of the first assembly 1999-2003 and has been included into the Welsh National Corpus Portal. A further corpus produced by the CATCymru project (CATCymru, 2009), covering the third assembly (2007-2010) has also been included into the Portal. Both corpora provide in total approximately 850,000 parallel segments and a word count of 20 million. Thus when added together these corpora have been a valuable resource for a wide spectrum of users from statistical machine translation practitioners to freelance translators who make heavy use of the portal's search facilities in conjunction with their terminology searches.

The National Assembly for Wales has streamlined and simplified its publication of the record. It also currently has a machine translation strategy with Microsoft to speed up the translation of the Assembly Record and lower costs. It is likely therefore that this particular collection in the corpus portal will grow substantially over the coming months and years.

3.4 The experimental language register corpus

This is a very small corpus extracted from the much larger but as yet unpublished Corpws Cysill Ar-lein (see 4.1). Its purpose is to study linguistic features of various language registers, especially with a view to developing methods of accurately tagging and recognizing texts according to their language register. This forms part of a Welsh Government and S4C project on speech recognition, but it is foreseen that a corpus of language registers will also be of much wider interest to the academic community. The corpus is still under development, but can already be accessed through the Welsh National Corpus Portal.

4 Unpublished corpora

4.1 The Cysill Ar-lein corpus

A special, free on-line version of a Welsh language spelling and grammar checker, Cysill (Cysill Ar-lein, 2009), was created with a view of collecting user generated samples of Welsh texts. This automatically generates a corpus of errors, with the corrected texts collected also from the users' sessions. The on-line version of Cysill has been very popular for a number of years. During four months of use in early 2014, the corpus grew by 2.5 million words, an average monthly total of 650,000 words of text throughput. To date the corpus comprises upwards of 14 million words each in corrected and uncorrected versions.

An analysis of the content shows a wide variety of text types, ranging from school and student essays to job applications, journalistic articles, formal documents, blogs, tweets and e-mails. Although use of this corpus for academic research was clearly stated in the terms and conditions, with warnings concerning privacy and confidentiality, sensitive material such as job applications and CVs containing names and addresses are common in it. Publication has been frustrated by users' lack of attention to these warnings, and it is inadvisable to publish without reasonable quality of anonymization. It is however available internally for research purposes, and has been used by staff and students, notably by Wooldridge (Wooldridge, 2011) in her MRes study of interference from English on Welsh texts.

4.2 The corpora of 19th century and World War I Welsh newspapers

The latter part of the nineteenth century and beginning of the twentieth century was the golden age of Welsh newspaper publishing. There was a large literate Welsh public who had not yet learnt English who supported a thriving Welsh language press. A recent project to create a website of resources for the First World War in Wales (Cymru 1914, [no date]), sponsored by JISC (a registered charity that champions the use of digital technologies in UK education and research), and led by the National Library of Wales, included a task to provide gist machine translation of the Welsh language newspapers into English. Unlike translations carried out to an accepted standard by human translators, gist translations only aim to provide a rough idea of the contents. They need not be polished in terms of language or always accurate in terms of meaning, but they provide a quick and cheap way to access source texts in a language which is unknown to the reader.

In order to complete this task, digitized copies of the Welsh newspapers from the war period were used, totalling approximately 11 million words. The much larger collection of digitized pre-war collection of Welsh newspapers, totalling approximately 223 million words was also received by the project, to be used as training data. Both these bodies of texts were imported into the Welsh National Corpus Portal infrastructure for ease of manipulation.

The quality of the digitization of these newspapers is not very high, due to the poor ink and paper quality. The unstandardized orthography and old fashioned language can also cause difficulties, and further work on this corpus could include the use of automatic standardization techniques similar to those used by Scannell (Scannell, 2009) for the Irish language. Nevertheless this could still be a very valuable corpus of Welsh, especially since it is by far the largest corpus of Welsh available. Efforts are currently under way to obtain permission to publish these corpora. In the meantime they are searchable internally and have been used in a chunking exercise to develop language models for speech technology and machine translation for Welsh.

6. Conclusion

The Welsh National Corpus Portal to date includes a corpus of contemporary academic Welsh, a legacy corpus of Welsh designed for word count and lexical purposes, a bilingual corpus of parliamentary Welsh, and an experimental corpus of different language registers. Adding to these the Cysill corpus of errors, and the nineteenth and early twentieth century newspaper corpora gives us an unexpectedly broad and deep range of Welsh language corpora. Given that only the DECHE corpus and experimental corpus of registers received any grant funding, and only as secondary considerations to other primary objectives, a great deal has been accomplished in recent years. Further work aims to expand the collection and integrate more natural Welsh language processing tools to aid annotation analysing and searching. It is hoped that the Welsh National Corpus Portal will continue to grow and provide inspiration for other less-resourced languages facing similar challenges.

References

Adam Kilgarrif, P. Rychly, P. Smrz, D. Tugwell. 2004. The Sketch Engine. *Proc EURALEX 2004, Lorient, France Pp. 105-116.* http://www.sketchengine.co.uk

CATCymru. 2009. *Cyfieithu â Chymorth Cyfrifiadur: Computer Assisted Translation.* [Online] Available at: http://www.catcymru.org/wordpress/?p=13043. [Accessed: 8 May 2014].

Coleg Cymraeg Cenedlaethol. 2011. *Coleg Cymraeg Cenedlaethol Academic Plan.* Available at: http://www.colegcymraeg.ac.uk/en/media/main/dogfennau-ccc/dogfennaucorfforaethol/CCCAcademicPlan.pdf [Accessed: 8 May 2014].

Cymru 1914. [No date]. *The Welsh Experience of the First World War* [Online] Available at: http://www.cymru1914.org [Accessed: 8 May 2014].

Cysill Ar-lein. 2009. *Welsh Spelling and Grammar Checker* [Online] Available at: http://www.cysgliad.com/cysill/arlein/ [Accessed: 8 May 2014].

Dafydd Jones & Andreas Eisele. 2006. Phrase-based Statistical Machine Translation between English and Welsh. *LREC Conference Proceedings.* Available at: http://www.mt-archive.info/LREC-2006-Jones.pdf [Accessed: 8 May 2014].

Dawn Wooldridge. 2011. *Gwella Cysill at Ddefnydd Cyfieithwyr: adnabod ymyrraeth agan yr iaith Saesneg mewn testunau Cymraeg.* MRes, Bangor University. Available at: http://www.cyfieithwyrcymru.org.uk/adnoddau-4.aspx [Accessed: 18 June 2014].

Kevin P. Scannell. 2007. *The Crúbadán Project: Corpus building for under-resourced languages.* [Online] Available at: http://borel.slu.edu/pub/wac3.pdf [Accessed: 9 May 2014].

Kevin P. Scannell. 2009. *Standardization of corpus texts for the New English-Irish Dictionary.* Paper presented at the 15th annual NAACLT conference, New York, 22 14 May 2009. Available at: http://borel.slu.edu/pub/naaclt09.pdf [Accessed: 18 June 2014].

Maristella Gatto. 2014. *Web as Corpus Theory and Practice.* Bloomsbury Academic.

N. C. Ellis, C. O'Dochartaigh, W. Hicks, M. Morgan, & N. Laporte. 2001. *Cronfa Electroneg o Gymraeg (CEG): A 1 million word lexical database and frequency count for Welsh.* [Online] Available at: http://www.bangor.ac.uk/canolfanbedwyr/ceg.php.en [Accessed: 8 May 2014].

Porth Termau Cenedlaethol Cymru. [No date]. *Welsh National Terminology Portal* [Online]. Available at: http://termau.org/?lang=en [Accessed: 8 May 2014].

Porth Corpora Cenedlaethol Cymru. [No date]. *Welsh National Corpus Portal* [Online]. Available at: http://www.corpws.org/?lang=en/ [Accessed: 8 May 2014].

Y Porth. [No date]. *Y Porth* [Online] Available at: https://www.porth.ac.uk/en/ [Accessed: 8 May 2014].

Subsegmental language detection in Celtic language text

Akshay Minocha
IIIT Hyderabad
Hyderabad (India)
akshay.minocha@students.iiit.ac.in

Francis M. Tyers
Giellatekno
UiT Norgga árktalaš universitehta
9017 Romsa (Norway)
francis.tyers@uit.no

Abstract

This paper describes an experiment to perform language identification on a sub-sentence basis. The typical case of language identification is to detect the language of documents or sentences. However, it may be the case that a single sentence or segment contains more than one language. This is especially the case in texts where *code switching* occurs.

1 Introduction

Determining the language of a piece of text is one of the first steps that must be taken before proceeding with further computational processing. This task has received a substantial amount of attention in recent years (Cavnar and Trenkle, 1994; Lui and Baldwin, 2012). However, previous research has on the whole assumed that a given text will be in a single language. When dealing with text from formal domains, this may be the case — although there are exceptions — such as quotations embedded in the text in another language. But when dealing with informal text, particularly in languages where the speech community is predominantly bi- or multi-lingual, this assumption may not hold.

The work presented in this paper was motivated by the problems in normalising non-standard input for the Celtic languages as a precursor to machine translation. When applying a normalisation strategy to a piece of text, it is necessary to first know the language of the piece of text you are applying it to.

The remainder of the paper is laid out as follows. In Section 3 we describe the problem in more detail and look at relevant prior work before proposing a novel method of sub-sentential language detection. Section 4 describes the evaluation methodology. Then in Section 5 we present the results of our method and compare it against several other possible methods. Finally, Section 6 presents future work and conclusions.

2 Related Work

Code-switching and segment detection problems have been the subject of previous research. A good deal of work has been done on detecting code-switched segments in speech data (Chan et al., 2004; Lyu et al., 2006). It is seen that language modelling techniques have shown promise earlier, such as in Yu et al. (2013), the experiment on Mandarin-Taiwanese sentences show a high accuracy in terms of detecting code-switched sentences.

In Chan et al. (2004) the authors have made use of the bi-phone probabilities and calculated them to measure a confidence metric, to (Lyu et al., 2006) which has made use of named syllable-based duration classification, which uses the tonal syllable properties along with the speech signals to help predict the code switch points. In Yeong and Tan (2010) the authors use syllable structure information to identify words in code-switched text in Malay-English, however they did not recognise segments in running text, only identifying individual words.

Proceedings of the First Celtic Language Technology Workshop, pages 76–80,
Dublin, Ireland, August 23 2014.

Pair	Language	Statistics (%)	
		Tokens	Segments
Irish—English	Irish	332	40
	English	379	42
Welsh—English	Welsh	419	64
	English	378	66
Breton—French	Breton	388	54
	French	379	53

Table 1: Document statistics of the annotated data used.

```
[en You're a] [ga Meiriceánach, cén fáth] [en are you] [ga foghlaim Gaeilge?!]
@afaltomkins [cy gorfod cael bach o tan] [en though init]
[en omg] [cy mar cwn bach yn] [en black and tan] [cy a popeth,] [en even cuter!!]
```

Figure 1: Example of text from a microblogging site chunked manually.

3 Methodology

As the number of possible languages for each segment is in theory the set of all the world's written languages, we take a decision to simplify the task by only looking at texts in the Celtic language and the corresponding majority language spoken where the Celtic language is spoken. That is, we looked at detecting between Irish and English, Welsh and English and Breton and French.

3.1 Corpus

We hand-annotated a small evaluation set from a selection of posts to a popular microblogging site.[1] The *tweets* (microblog posts) were filtered into three sets which had been identified as Irish, Welsh and Breton using the *langid* tool (Lui and Baldwin, 2012). From these, we manually selected between 40 and 50 tweets for each language pair. Statistics on the number of segments and tokens is presented in Table 1. Certain tokens were escaped from the data, such as the 'mentioned' character (`@` symbol), subject tags 'hashtags' which are preceded by a # symbol, hyperlinks and the sequence `rt` which stands for 're-tweet'. An example of the content of our corpus after hand annotation is given in Figure 1. All of the tweets had at least one instance of code-switching.

3.2 Alphabet n-gram approach

We use the character n-gram approach along with some heuristics which are relevant to our problem domain of identifying segments for subsequent processing. We would like to both predict the code switched points but looking at the surrounding structure also decide the inclusion of them into the current or the next segment.

We first built character language models using IRSTLM (Federico et al., 2008) for the five languages in question. For English and French a model was trained using the EuroParl corpus (Koehn, 2005). For Breton, Welsh and Irish we used corpora of text crawled from the web. To ensure no bias and also since our dataset for Breton was around 1.5 million, we sampled the same size of data for all the five languages. In order to build a character language model we replaced spaces with the underscore symbol '_', and then placed a space character between each character. Punctuation and non-letter characters are also part of this language model. For example, the word 'sláinte!' would be broken down into a sequence of {'_ s', 's l', 'l á', 'á i', 'i n', 'n t', 't e', 'e !', '! _'}.

3.3 Sequence chunking

This section describes the way we apply heuristics to segment and label the input text. In Figure 2, 'chunks' represent the list of evaluated tuples of segments and their labelled language, 'buffer' is the expanding segment. LANGPREDICT corresponds to any function which is used to determine the language

[1] `http://indigenoustweets.blogspot.in/2013/12/mapping-celtic-twittersphere.html`

of the token. The flag variable helps in implementing the heuristic of minimum segment size while labelling chunks.

```
Require: s : sentence to chunk
buffer = [ ] /*Undecided expanding window of chunk*/
chunks = [ ] /*Decided labelled segment*/
buffer_language ← LANGPREDICT(s[0]) /* Language of first word */
flag ← 0
for all w ∈ s do
    if LANGPREDICT(w)=buffer_language then
        if flag = 1 then
            buffer ← buffer + [word_buffer,w]
            flag ← 0
        else
            buffer ← buffer + [ w]
    if LANGPREDICT(w) ≠buffer_language then
        if flag= 0 then
            flag ← 1
            word_buffer ← w
            continue
        else
            chunks ← chunks + [(buffer,buffer_language)]
            buffer ← [word_buffer,w]
            buffer_language ← LANGPREDICT(w) /* Language of new expanding chunk */
            flag ← 0
if length(buffer) ≠0 then
    chunks ← chunks + [(buffer,buffer_language)]
```

Figure 2: Chunking Algorithm

3.4 Word-based prediction

Designed keeping in mind importance of the most common words, this procedure included checking each word against both of the word lists in question,[2] it is associated to one language or another. In case of a conflict, for example, when the word exists in both wordlists, or in the case that it is unknown to both, the option of continuing with the previous span was taken and the previous selected tag was labelled, thus increasing the chunk.

3.5 Word-based prediction with character backoff

In case of the word being present in only one of the two monolingual word lists the classification is simple, but in case of a conflict, a character bigram backoff was introduced to help us disambiguate the language label.

4 Evaluation

For the Evaluation procedure, we follow the footsteps of the CoNLL-2000 shared task on language-independent named entity recognition: dividing text into syntactically related non-overlapping groups of words. This chunking mechanism (Tjong Kim Sang and De Meulder, 2003) is very similar to ours, in terms of words which only belong to one category (here, language), and also evaluation based on the segment structure present in the data. The chunks here are such that they belong to only one language.

The evaluation statistics shown in Tables 2 and 3 mention two values for each of the experiment conducted on the three bilingual language datasets. The first, is the percentage of correctly detected phrases, which is the overall precision and the second is the number of phrases in the data that were found by the chunker, which is the overall recall.

Apart from the techniques discussed in Section 3, some baselines are also used to give a comparative view of how well all the mechanisms perform.

4.1 Baseline

We used the language identification tool `langid.py` (Lui and Baldwin, 2012) on the whole dataset and labelled all the individual lines according to this majority classification. As no chunking is performed we

[2]For the wordlists we used the *aspell* wordlists widely available on Unix systems.

System		Irish—English		Welsh—English		Breton—French	
		Irish	English	Welsh	English	Breton	French
`baseline`	p	2.50	0.0	0.0	0.0	0.0	0.0
	r	2.56	0.0	0.0	0.0	0.0	0.0
`langid-3character`	p	5.00	14.29	0.0	21.21	1.85	20.75
	r	5.41	8.45	0.0	14.58	1.92	12.36
`wordlist`	p	32.50	28.57	26.69	**40.91**	57.41	33.96
	r	23.64	26.09	**26.03**	**33.75**	47.69	33.33
`character bigram`	p	32.50	35.71	23.44	19.70	57.41	52.83
	r	22.41	26.79	15.31	16.67	41.33	37.84
`wordlist+character bigram`	p	**52.50**	**50.00**	**32.81**	31.82	**70.37**	**67.92**
	r	**38.18**	**43.75**	24.14	25.61	**57.58**	**57.14**

Table 2: Precision, p and recall, r for the systems by language.

System	Accuracy (%)		
	Irish—English	Welsh—English	Breton—French
`baseline`	42.76	42.16	44.07
`langid-3character`	57.24	45.92	43.16
`wordlist`	79.75	**74.28**	83.96
`character bigram`	81.29	65.62	76.79
`wordlist+character bigram`	**85.79**	72.40	**88.79**

Table 3: Accuracy of the systems over the three language pairs. The accuracy measures how often a token was assigned to the right language, independent of span.

can expect that the precision and recall will be very low. However it does provide a reasonable baseline for the per-word accuracy.

4.2 `langid` character trigram prediction

For this system we used the character trigram probabilities to predict the detected language for each token. Trigrams were chosen after experimenting with 1–5 grams. The heuristics in Section 3 were followed for the text processing and chunking part of the method.

5 Results

As described in Section 3 the data collected from Twitter for the three language pairs, was processed using the techniques mentioned. The statistics of the same are given in Table 1.

While the precision and recall are low for the remaining models, we see that we are able to improve The performance by combining the wordlist based model with a character bigram model. And what is more, we are able to begin to not only identify particular words in a language, but also segments.

6 Conclusions

This paper has presented a very preliminary investigation into subsegment language identification in Celtic language texts. We have proposed a model that chunks input text into segments and performs language identification on these segments at the same time. Precision and recall are low, leaving a lot of room for further work. Although King and Abney (2013) label on a per word level, yet we would like to include supervised methods and features talked about in this research to improve our efficiency while dealing with segments. We would also like to attempt our method using higher order character n-gram models for backoff, and n-gram word language models for detection and on more annotated data.

Acknowledgements

We thank Kevin Scannell for help with providing data from Twitter and for useful comments and suggestions. This work was undertaken as part of the Apertium project in the 2014 Google Summer of Code.

References

William B Cavnar and John M Trenkle. 1994. N-gram-based text categorization. *Ann Arbor MI*, 48113(2):161–175.

Joyce YC Chan, PC Ching, Tan Lee, and Helen M Meng. 2004. Detection of language boundary in code-switching utterances by bi-phone probabilities. In *Chinese Spoken Language Processing, 2004 International Symposium on*, pages 293–296. IEEE.

Marcello Federico, Nicola Bertoldi, and Mauro Cettolo. 2008. Irstlm: an open source toolkit for handling large scale language models. In *Interspeech*, pages 1618–1621.

Ben King and Steven P Abney. 2013. Labeling the languages of words in mixed-language documents using weakly supervised methods. In *HLT-NAACL*, pages 1110–1119.

Philipp Koehn. 2005. Europarl: A parallel corpus for statistical machine translation. In *MT summit*, volume 5, pages 79–86.

Marco Lui and Timothy Baldwin. 2012. langid. py: An off-the-shelf language identification tool.

Dau-cheng Lyu, Ren-yuan Lyu, Yuang-chin Chiang, and Chun-nan Hsu. 2006. Language identification by using syllable-based duration classification on code-switching speech. In *Chinese Spoken Language Processing*, pages 475–484. Springer.

Erik F Tjong Kim Sang and Fien De Meulder. 2003. Introduction to the CoNLL-2003 shared task: Language-independent named entity recognition. In *Proceedings of the seventh conference on Natural language learning at HLT-NAACL 2003-Volume 4*, pages 142–147. Association for Computational Linguistics.

Yin-Lai Yeong and Tien-Ping Tan. 2010. Language identification of code switching malay-english words using syllable structure information. *Spoken Languages Technologies for Under-Resourced Languages (SLTU'10)*, pages 142–145.

Liang-Chih Yu, Wei-Cheng He, Wei-Nan Chien, and Yuen-Hsien Tseng. 2013. Identification of code-switched sentences and words using language modeling approaches. *Mathematical Problems in Engineering*, 2013.

Author Index